Strategic
Executive
Succession

Steven Salmi, PhD, LP
Founder and CEO, Corporate Psychologists

STRATEGIC EXECUTIVE SUCCESSION

ISBN: 978-0-9981779-4-6

Printed in the United States of America

Designed by Ivan Stojic

First Printing: 2019

This is a work of non-fiction. However, I have changed the names and identifying characteristics of many of the individuals in this book to disguise their identities.

Published by Corporate Psychologists, Inc.
in collaboration with Artisan Digital.

www.ArtisanDigital.org
(651) 600-0178

Contents

CHAPTER ONE
Succession Readiness 5

CHAPTER TWO
Maximum Momentum 21

CHAPTER THREE
Company | Plan 35

CHAPTER FOUR
Company | Successor 49

CHAPTER FIVE
Company | Practicalities 65

CHAPTER SIX
Customers | Retention 83

CHAPTER SEVEN
Customers | Connections 97

CHAPTER EIGHT
Customers | Handoff 111

CHAPTER NINE
Self | Identity 123

CHAPTER TEN
Self | Relationships 139

CHAPTER ELEVEN
Self | Purpose 153

Epilogue 165

Acknowledgements 167

CHAPTER ONE

Succession Readiness

M ike glances out his office window at the headlights of evening traffic choking his route home from the company he founded years ago. As he checks off a few more tasks before leaving, his progress is as slow-going as the vehicles creeping outside.

His mind is elsewhere. *What next?*

Mike knows that no one in his family, the next generation, wants to participate in the business, much less lead it. He loves his employees—most of them—but no one inside has emerged to take his place. And whenever outside buyers have come along, he's spurned them.

Early on, when Mike began pondering his own long-term plans, he would think out loud, making casual remarks at work or home that were inevitably interpreted as final decisions, triggering all kinds of unwanted disruption. Once or twice he had cultivated a competent lieutenant, a trusted sounding board and possible successor, who ended up exiting the organization before a transition could take place.

Nowadays, Mike carefully chooses what he says where—and when—and to whom. He keeps his thoughts mostly to himself.

Mike recently took a major step forward when he initiated a process to begin exploring his exit. He assembled a team of outside advisors— attorney, accountant, talent management expert—to quietly help the company toward a valuation where he feels good about letting go. He's not committed to a specific date or milestone for selling, instead looking out a few years to a prime window.

As Mike compares notes with other leaders—diverse founder/owners as well as CEOs of organizations with other structures—he knows he's tightening the right nuts and bolts for a sale.

That process, however, leaves his personal questions unanswered.

Now what?

Mike and his advisors have discussed creating a corporate board to inject fresh energy and ideas for growth. Mike could stay in command and chair the new board. Or step out of leadership but maintain his investment in the company. Or stake out some middle ground of shared responsibility, like Mike reporting to a strong, capable board.

No way. No bosses.

Mike assumes that ultimately a larger company or private equity firm will buy him out. They'll write him a big check and he'll go on his way, with no further connection to the business. The buyer might want him around for a while, but he can't see staying for long. As Mike contemplates a sale, he's looking for more than money. He wants the company to continue the family feel he's cultivated. But he doesn't have much control over that legacy, right?

I need to let go.

Truth be told, Mike wishes he could sell to someone who gets it, who would just let him hang around and come and go as he pleases.

Leaders Going

It's one of leadership's most enormous questions—What's the best time to move on, to allow someone else to lead the organization, to step into life after business? And, in the case of owners—What's the best moment to sell? **Even so, few leaders have an explicit exit plan. If they do, it's not likely as well thought-out as they think:**

- **Two-thirds of US public** and private companies admit they lack a formal CEO succession plan.[1]

- Two-thirds of executives at companies with a succession roadmap express dissatisfaction with the plan.[2]

When it comes to privately-owned businesses,

- Nearly 90 percent of organizations have no written plan to transition from the current owner.

- 80 percent of owners have never sought advice about a transition, apparently planning to go it alone.[3]

As a business owner and talent management expert, I'm not surprised by that data. But really? Planning for succession is critical, because the top leader's exit is a pivot point. At a pivot point, everything either goes forward or backward. There's no staying in place. That rule applies always, all the time, to every leader, in every type of organization. Stakeholders inside and outside the organization watch for what comes next. And the decisions in this process have immense consequences for the leader's own future.

When leaders say they have a plan, there's often not much there. It might be "I'm going to appoint Bob as my successor." Or any movements toward the exit are merely tactical, as in "I need an accountant to look at taxes. I'll get a lawyer to look at liability."

Most leaders recognize the need to map their steps. But they don't know how to develop a holistic strategic succession plan that achieves the best for their company, their customer, and their own future.

Leaders Staying

Perhaps you know a leader or two who will die at their desk, eating a greasy cheeseburger. Running the business is all they know. It's all they do. It's all they are.

These outliers aside, most executives understand that sooner or later, everyone leaves the business. Real willingness to think about your own exit, however, is another matter. As more than one leader has told me, "I'm not ready to go there." I've seen many leaders slam hard and fast into this mental barrier: **Executives are completely accustomed to knowing where they're going with the organization and what they want to accomplish. Thinking about what comes next for the business or for themselves—and not seeing it clearly—that's unsettling.**

Statistics on Succession Readiness might feel irrelevant to your situation. Maybe you have the option and desire to stay in your role indefinitely, and you think, "I'm never going to leave." Or "I can't imagine wanting to sell."

As someone who makes a living getting inside the thinking of leaders, I'd ask if you're honestly assessing the situation.

If you are—and you still conclude you're not ready—that's great. I love my work, and I hope you do too. I can understand if you have unfinished business. Goals to achieve. If you still gain purpose, satisfaction, and enjoyment from your work, there truly might be nothing that could pull you away.

In fact, if you're a business builder, the very idea of ever being done with work might put you on edge. If you leave, what's left? What's the alternative? What will you do with your drive?

Your role models might include heroes who died in the saddle. When people say the words "next season" or "retirement," you hear "slow, agonizing death, marked by extreme boredom."

This mindset means you'll probably watch friends retire, years or decades before you begin to think about a change. Others in your professional and personal circles will talk on and on about their great new life, and they'll press you to quit and join them. But for you, retirement doesn't have the same cachet.

Plenty of leaders share your perspective. It can feel significantly out of step with society's accepted values and timetables.

Importantly, if you were to leave your leadership role without a readiness plan, a solid idea of what lies ahead, you would put yourself at high risk of frustration and regret. There's a good chance you would boomerang back to a leadership or owner role, possibly enduring heavy financial, relational, and emotional losses in your exit and reentry. I've seen it.

If you're not ready, stay put. For now. But keep reading.

Leaders Stuck

Consciously choosing to stay in your leadership role is far different from being stuck.

Stuck shows up in a lot of ways. Leaders might simply be ready to be out of the business but haven't done the necessary preparation to leave. Or loved ones might be prodding them to be done with work, but they simply don't know what comes next.

I've observed three especially difficult categories of stuck:

Identity—I Am My Work
Some leaders are so tied to position and organization that in practical terms, the outside world doesn't exist. They

have few relationships outside work. Over time, their external commitments, interests, and hobbies have waned. They make no effort to enlarge their world.

Duty—I Have a Job to Do

Other leaders stay in the business because anything else would feel like a betrayal of people past, present, and future. This burden of responsibility is common in family businesses but can happen anywhere. The burned-out leader goes through the motions without energy to advance the organization. Employees who expect more drift away, and a slow organizational decline sets in.

Ego—I Am Irreplaceable

Ego-driven leaders think no one in the world possesses the knowledge or experience needed to do their job. They delegate with difficulty, and they end up micromanaging their disempowered, underdeveloped people. Creating overly dependent employees fuels the dynamic and feeds the narrative that the leader is indispensable.

Stuck leaders don't develop the business. They don't innovate. They become dinosaurs. By failing to change in a volatile world, they become easy targets for their competition.

Leaders who stay past their prime damage the business in real time. They also sabotage the future by failing to create an organization able to sustain itself beyond their presence.

When leaders are truly stuck—driven by identity, duty, or ego—it's nearly impossible for them to think and act productively around succession. They need first to become aware of and begin working through those underlying issues.

Your Next Steps

Leaders often sense danger in considering what comes next. They fear getting burned.

If you've raised the succession issue in the past, maybe nothing good came of it. Or you worry that saying out loud that someday you might be done initiates a doomsday countdown. That all-or-nothing thinking doesn't hold up. Wanting to understand the issues around a strategic exit doesn't mean you have to leave anytime soon. Having a robust Succession Readiness plan can help you avoid being forced into a premature departure or panic sale.

You might be able to live with ambiguity about what comes next, but others really want and need to know what lies ahead. Lack of planning means uncertainty for the company, for customers, and for loved ones. Uncertainty is a painful place to live, and leaders can miss the full impact of their indecision on others.

If you don't know what comes next for you, I want to invite you to explore the possibilities and what it takes to get there.

I'm a business person first, with a deep specialization in talent. Just as some leaders focus on organizational finance or strategy, I work on the people side of business. My training and experience as a psychologist means I often see the dynamics of people, relationships, and motivations more keenly than others.

In my experience as a psychologist, talent management expert, and succession coach, my 25 years of watching leaders navigate transition is the best education I've ever had. Working around the table with leaders—their successors—as well as accountants and attorneys, I've learned there are no simple answers on these topics. Every situation skews a little from the others. Different concerns, different answers.

I know you're busy. Contrary to stereotypes of executive leaders, you have NOT been putting yourself first, or you might not want or need this book. While I can't foresee every detail of your next move, I know the main themes and the right questions to ask to help you get ready. I can help backfill gaps in your knowledge and give you frameworks for defining your own needs. I will help you wrap your head around a transition that might be years out.

Succession Readiness

There are no decisions for you to make right now, other than choosing to explore what a transition means for your company, your customers, and yourself. There are no commitments, other than wanting to be ready when your best moment comes along.

You've heard countless times that "You should have a good succession plan." And suppose you pick a successor. Why that person? What's the strategy? What exactly do you expect him or her to accomplish that will move the organization forward now and for years to come?

Leaders of all stripes sense something isn't right, but their current knowledge around strategic succession isn't enough to move them forward.

For example, I know that most owners looking toward the exit aren't well equipped for the transition. For all but a few, selling a business will be a one-and-done activity. Serial entrepreneurs walk in and out of ownership multiple times, but most leaders start or buy a single business, develop it over time, and in their final phases face decisions they've never made before.

The usual advice is to seek out an accountant or a lawyer, who will tell you what to do. That's a start, but it only meets a portion of your needs. Relying solely on financial and legal professionals can addresses dollars and legalities, but it neglects the people and personal sides.

As you exit a leadership role, you need a holistic approach that answers the following questions:

- **Is my talent ready?**

- **Are my customers on board?**

- **What will I do next?**

I call this holistic approach not a succession *plan* but Succession Readiness. Too often plans are conceived, documented, and shelved. Readiness is a state to attain, maintain, and execute.

About This Book

Succession Readiness isn't a bullet-point list for your exit but a comprehensive approach to achieving the best for your company, your customers, and your own future.

My talent management practice, Corporate Psychologists, serves organizations from start-ups to companies in the Fortune 50. We collaborate with organizations to create systematic, customized programs for workforce planning, forecasting, and action. This wise, efficient deployment of key players and people at all levels results in heightened confidence throughout the business.

We bring our experience across organizations to a special focus on executive and CEO succession in small- to mid-size companies and non-profits.

As I work with exiting leaders, I notice a palpable sense of history and legacy. They want answers to weighty questions like:

- What did I do with this organization on my watch?

- Did I move the company forward? Did it grow? Where is it still lacking?

- How well did I provide for my family?

- Who else did I help? Are my employees and their families well cared for?

- What will be left after I leave?

- How will people remember me?

- What happens now?

Good leaders know their decisions have consequences. They feel the weight of every judgment. They want to look back on their work with pride and satisfaction and say, "I did well with the time I had." That value doesn't vanish when it comes time to exit. It only intensifies.

This book is for leaders who care about leaving well—those who believe that how they exit matters not just for themselves but for their organization and the customers they serve.

The comprehensive Succession Readiness I describe here lets you add value even as you leave—*especially* as you leave. And that's what people will remember. How did you prepare the organization? Was it ready? Did it prosper after you left?

My focus here is on executives with several core characteristics:

- **They exercise BROAD LEADERSHIP.** They make directional decisions for an entire organization or possess significant span of control over a division or function.

- **They retain RESPONSIBILITY for what happens next.** Their situation allows involvement in the succession process, including onboarding their replacement and strengthening customer relationships through the transition.

- **They likely have a FINANCIAL STAKE in the organization.** Their departure will impact their ownership or other compelling financial interest.

- **They care about a POWERFUL LEGACY.** Their emotional ownership of their work means they want the organization to thrive long after their leaving.

- **They desire PERSONAL PREPARATION for what comes next.** I'm concerned about leaders who count on figuring out their future once they get there. That's like buying supplies and boarding up your windows after a hurricane makes landfall.

I work with leaders and those who surround them, so the topics I address will be helpful to boards and others assisting in the succession process. They will inform other executives, partners, stakeholders and shareholders, and participants in a family business.

I do a significant portion of my coaching and training with entrepreneurs, high potentials on the rise, and teams at the top, and for them this book relays useful information on how transitions *should* happen, including leaving a position where they have made a significant personal investment. Its insights cover building people, bringing successors along, and handing off responsibilities. It shows how to work yourself out of a job by preparing your replacement to take over.

A leader's loved ones who thumb through this book will get an easy-to-read feel for what a departing executive faces.

Fine print: This book doesn't provide detailed instructions on how to sell your business. Or address legal contingencies. Or manage wealth post-transition. And it isn't a self-help guide to unknotting the relational dynamics of family ownership. My goal is to describe strategic executive succession from a talent management perspective.

Bottom Line: Good Business

Whether you're enthusiastic about Succession Readiness or still thinking "I'm not ready to go there," let me add that running a good business means ensuring you keep your options open. You don't have to decide to exit your leadership role anytime soon. But you keep all options alive by creating an environment where you're ready for your big moment when it arrives. Missing out on opportunities because you've decided *not* to be prepared—that puts a lot at risk.

The succession-ready leader can affirmatively state, "I've created an organization ready for whatever opportunities present themselves." That's just good business.

By doing anything less, you dramatically increase the risk of

- Frustration for you

- Failure for your successor

- Fall-off for your organization

Whether you're a CEO, owner, or other executive leader, inadequate preparation for your succession means you'll fail to reap the full rewards of the seeds you planted. If your succession isn't managed well, what remains is diminished for everyone.

At Risk—Legacy

For many leaders, their most important legacy isn't the finely-tuned structures and positive P&L statements they leave behind but how they'll be remembered. If the transition process seems random or reckless, jilted employees will say of the leader, "Oh, he took the money and ran. He left us in the dust." Far better for those employees to be able to say, "This is a thoughtful process. It's well managed. We're set up for success. Now it's up to us. We'll be okay."

At Risk—Organizational Survival

If employee confidence tanks, productivity inevitably drops, people across the organization start polishing resumes, and key employees flee. Especially in an economic, industry, or local environment where other options exist, the best talent always finds a way out. Couple a talent departure with bad business decisions made by a poorly-chosen successor, and the organization can collapse. For example, of family businesses transitioning to second-generation ownership, only 30% survive.[4]

At Risk—Financial Stake

Owners who fail in the discipline of Succession Readiness inevitably lose business valuation points. Whatever the expected price multiples in an industry, succession preparedness or lack of it can substantially increase or decrease those multiples. If an owner continues a financial connection after investing many years in a business—and now manages this last decision poorly—a lifetime of work can be erased.

At Risk—Personal Well-Being

Some retired leaders just look old—the gray hair, the way they carry themselves, the dramatic aging. Not long ago I spotted one leader who left the role he loved for a life without much going on. He walks the dog a lot—good for the dog, not enough for him. There's an awareness and genuine fear among executives of statistics about retired leaders who depart, dry up, and die. Without giving real thought to what comes next for you personally, the future you want will elude you.

Your Next Great Act

Some have called a leader's departure the "last great act." That makes sense if succession happens to be a leader's final major organizational decision. It's like a coach's last championship or a composer's magnum opus. But I would hope exiting an organization or selling a business isn't your last great act. That's depressing. It's enough to make any leader feel like staying forever.

I've seen many senior leaders energized, however, by creating a future that maximizes possibilities for the organization, customers, and themselves. They get electrified when they

- Create an organization healthy enough to thrive in a transition

- Choose and onboard a leader well-matched to organizational leadership needs for now and for the future

- Get customers onboard with new leadership and refreshed commitment to relationships

- Set the organization up for success not just for what it's been but what it will be

Moreover, leaders who find their own purpose beyond the organization discover that their need to hang around and exert control diminishes. They see into their own future and plunge forward.

I hope in this moment you find the courage to begin moving toward your next great act—to enter this process and what comes next.

Succession Readiness isn't an end. It's the path to where you go next. Let's see where it takes you.

Endnotes

1   2016–2017 NACD Public Company Governance Survey, National Association of Corporate Directors, https://www.nacdonline.org/insights/publications.cfm?ItemNumber=37388 (accessed May 31, 2019).

2   Spencer Stuart, Stats from PWC PDF on succession planning. Of the executives who told headhunter Korn Ferry this year that their companies do have such a program, only 1/3 were satisfied with the outcome.

3   Mary Ellen Biery, "Study Shows Why Many Business Owners Can't Sell When They Want To," *Forbes.com*, February 5, 2017, https://www.forbes.com/sites/sageworks/2017/02/05/these-8-stats-show-why-many-business-owners-cant-sell-when-they-want-to/#1664c6b44bd5 (accessed May 31, 2019).

4   Claudio Fernández-Aráoz, Sonny Iqbal, and Jörge Ritter, "Leadership Lessons from Great Family Businesses," *Harvard Business Review*, April 2015, https://hbr.org/2015/04/leadership-lessons-from-great-family-businesses (accessed May 31, 2019).

CHAPTER TWO

Maximum Momentum

Sharon leaned back in her desk chair, contemplating news that had just broken. A leadership counterpart—CEO of her closest competitor—had been tersely dismissed. While his departure created business opportunities for her own organization, for the moment, personal implications hit harder. Sharon was certain she was secure in her position as leader of a mid-size manufacturer, but the CEO's forced exit felt like yet another cautionary example.

Sharon was hired as an engineer into her organization in her late 20s. She was busy deepening her technical prowess when the owner of what was then a small shop chose her to lead business development, hoping she could nudge the business past a plateau.

Enthused by a bigger sandbox to play in and confident she couldn't do any worse than her predecessors, Sharon reached out to expand and diversify the company's customer base. It was soon obvious she was an extraordinary salesperson. Leveraging her specialist background, she became a bridge between customers and engineering and drove multiple new product lines. The firm grew exponentially, and when it was purchased by investors, she assumed an interim COO role. She remained COO until she was named CEO a few years later.

Everything Sharon has touched bears her mark, and the news of her counterpart made her even more resolute not to allow what she has built to be torn from her.

Now, in her early 60s, Sharon is still 115% buzzed about what she does each day. The business is financially sound, and lawyers have seen to every legal concern. Her owners still value her work, and the community loves her for building one of the area's leading employers.

When Sharon pauses to reflect, she knows her head and heart are still in the business, but her energy won't last forever. Her husband grumbles about her inability to get away for extended breaks, and their grandchildren are growing up too quickly. After months of serious thought, Sharon commits to herself and her family that she'll begin to work her way out of the business, knowing that will require a final push of time and energy to ensure the ongoing success of what everyone has sacrificed to build.

Sharon answers to an active ownership team, so decisions about her future aren't completely in her control. But she's determined to go out on top.

Finishing Well

In my experience, leaders feel a very human mix of thoughts and emotions about leaving an organization. Those who love their work and have much to celebrate feel twangs of sadness anticipating missing their team, customers, or pet business projects. Others who are desperate to be done still feel pride of achievement in how far they've brought the organization, sometimes with flashes of anger that they can't keep going. This ambivalence seldom changes the overall dynamic. When it's time to go, it's time to go. Most leaders just know.

I've observed two interconnected realities about exiting leaders:

LEADERSHIP OBSERVATION 1:
LEADERS DON'T STAY FOREVER.

LEADERSHIP OBSERVATION 2:
LEADERS RARELY GO OUT ON TOP.

Remarkably few leaders fully achieve what they want as they wind down their service and look toward whatever comes next. Why? They delay thinking about their transition. They let circumstances determine their path. They miss opportunities. They fail to envision their own future.

Lack of Succession Readiness spoils the exit of many leaders. The best transitions happen when intention meets execution. Going out on top isn't accidental.

Great transitions start with a leader's habit of continually building and strengthening the organization. The leader's decisions, including those about moving on, are grounded in thoughtful reflection and safeguarded by expert counsel. The run-up to the exit injects a burst of activity that gives the leader's work the best chance of enduring, including make-or-break efforts like choosing and onboarding a successor and cementing relationships between the new leader and existing customers. For owners, the additional task of preparing for a sale requires tightening down financial and legal matters as well as opening communication with potential buyers. As all of this happens, exiting leaders simultaneously begin to explore and test ideas of their own life after business.

The leader who continues to grow the organization until the last day on the job—while preparing for his or her future—is the leader most likely go out on top with energy to spare for what's next.

For some leaders, that scenario sounds unworkable. They're starting to lose steam, and maybe the business needs another investment of energy or creativity they just can't deliver. They know they can't stand still—the business grows or dies, and they know they can't grow it. They try to get by in maintenance mode, and a slow decay might set in. At some point, they conclude, "I just don't have the energy to get the business to the next level."

I hear that a lot.

But Succession Readiness is attainable.

Whatever your current situation, this book is your guide to focusing on the most important issues.

Leadership Exit Scenarios

Ready or not, all leaders wonder about the best time to exit. In your own thinking, one of the following categories of when and why leaders go might stand out, or several factors might play a part.

Milestone Exit

There's no longer a magic age when leaders are supposed to leave, and the traditional milestone of retirement at 65 is no longer the norm. Exiting leaders can be young or old, and to the extent that age is a driver, the milestone is usually more than a simple number. It can be tied to events like getting the kids through college. Or it can be a milestone in other key relationships, such as a spouse retiring and wanting you present to fulfill long-postponed dreams. I've noticed that if leaders are still fully engaged at age 65 to 70, they often hang on a bit longer.

Milestones are problematic. It's nearly impossible to set a hard target date.

If you work for someone else, the timing isn't your call, and bosses likely care little about the flip of a calendar. If you're an owner, you can't just put a date out there and do business as usual and expect buyers to line up on demand. You can't think, "Okay, I hit 65. Now I'm going to entertain offers." Buyers will come along and say, "You're not ready. You've got two years of work before this organization is ready for the market." Buyers don't care whether you're 65 or 85. They want to buy an organization prepared for transition. The buyer must perceive the business has been readied for sale.

Distress Exit

A distress exit is a tipping point where you believe you have little choice but to be done. You're depleted, dead-ended, and looking for the door. Here are a few distress-exit scenarios I've observed, followed by key thoughts on how you might find your way forward:

- **HEALTH** – Concerns about your own health or a loved one's well-being can strike at any time and without warning. Medical crises are a prime reason for leaders curtailing responsibilities or exiting on short notice.

- **FAMILY** – Pressure at home frequently pushes leaders toward the exit. Critical responsibilities can reach a breaking point. Or a spouse just says, "I have my own dreams of getting away and seeing the world" or "I want to visit the grandkids more often. How long are you going to keep this up?" It prompts a serious reevaluation of how you should spend the next few years.

- **EXTERNAL DISRUPTORS** – Leaders might decide to exit when they face a major change in the way business is done. A black swan in the economy or competitive disruption comes along and a leader asks, "Are we even relevant anymore?" It takes enormous energy to reinvent and go on.

- **INTERNAL OBSTACLES** – Leaders can face diverse internal reasons to be done. For some, the fun is simply gone. Or the thrill of achievement has died. Or doing what you've done in the past no longer moves you forward. Working harder and longer doesn't help. Frustrated, you turn inward—and get anxious or depressed. Or outward—and blame others for your situation. Either can signal a need to transition.

- **PEOPLE FATIGUE** – Burnout over people issues is probably the most common reason for a distress exit. You just get tired of dealing with it all. The worst kind of people fatigue comes in the form of betrayal. Someone in your inner circle steals from you. Or leaves and takes customers with them. Or turns the team against you. Those circumstances can make anyone want to hang it up.

Finding yourself in a distress scenario doesn't mean you're washed up or that exiting is your only option. You've recovered from countless crises. Perhaps you can do it again.

When you sense your leadership energy on the wane, it's crucial to seek help sooner rather than later. If your core team and others in your organization can't help you forward, look for outside assistance. Your trusted advisors might have fresh ideas for addressing your challenges, and an extreme situation might push you to consider options thus far out of bounds. In the talent management realm, an executive coach might be able to step in and help individuals or groups create breakthroughs. On a more personal front, seeing a counselor might be a good idea to help you cope with stress.

Whatever you do, don't put exploring succession on hold until you find your way out of the distress. The impulse to conserve energy and focus on immediate issues is understandable, but down the road you may have even less resilience.

The danger of delaying is that you let transition preparations slide until your choices become limited and you feel forced to exit or sell with no notice. You don't want to be in a place where you wake up one day and decide you're done. You're almost guaranteed to make reactive decisions that aren't in your best interest.

Interestingly, the process of developing Succession Readiness can impart an energizing jolt—a reignited business imagination, organizational vision, or entrepreneurial spirit.

As you look back at how far you've come, you might discover fresh energy to move forward. At least you'll be more clearheaded as you decide between "I want to do this a while longer" and "I want to be done and put my energy elsewhere."

If you've climbed the corporate ladder, you're accustomed to changing roles and organizations. If you're the owner of a firm you built from little or nothing, you likely can't imagine working anywhere else—if you're out, you're done. Whatever your career path up to this point, don't rule out a leadership role elsewhere. Some distressed leaders go on to join other organizations. Or start new ones. And some indeed come to the point where they embrace their own version of retirement, whatever that looks like. If you still have gas in the tank, don't let anyone tell you what you can or can't do. Keep your options open.

Opportunity Exit

Opportunities come and go, but the crucial question is this: What makes an opportunity a real possibility—or the obvious choice? The more you can think through who you are and what you want to do, the more likely you'll reach a clearheaded conclusion—and the less likely you'll commit to actions you later regret.

Leadership exit opportunities are created by mergers and acquisitions, incentives, buy-outs, and more. Some opportunities come with a dark twist. Suppose you're forced out. Someone who doesn't like your work offers you money to go away. Consider that an opportunity. Worse things can happen. It's tough to have upward success and then feel like you've failed at the last thing you do. Realistically, however, half of all executive gigs don't end well. If your future with an organization is at risk, work hard to finish well for as long as you can, then shift to finding your path post-exit.

Owners consider a maximum value sale to be the ultimate opportunity. They dream of a big buyout, with multiple suitors at the door begging to write a jumbo check. I won't disagree with that. I will repeat what I've already said. For most owners, the ideal sale also continues their legacy. The secret is knowing how to get both.

Maximum Momentum

The ultimate opportunity exit for all leaders is what I call "Maximum Momentum."

Succession Readiness is your continual movement toward your best opportunity. Maximum Momentum is the strategic framework to optimize outcomes for your company, your customers, and your own future.

The best executive succession results from gaining and growing momentum across all parts of the process. In fact, I've never seen a successful leadership succession where all interests haven't been addressed and advanced. You can visualize these Maximum Momentum components as a triangle:

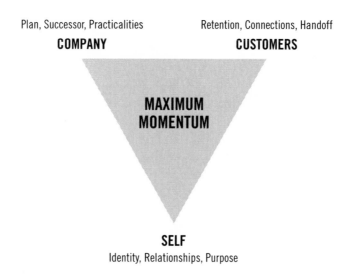

| Plan, Successor, Practicalities | Retention, Connections, Handoff |
| **COMPANY** | **CUSTOMERS** |

MAXIMUM MOMENTUM

SELF
Identity, Relationships, Purpose

THE MAXIMUM MOMENTUM TRIANGLE

Each component of Maximum Momentum spotlights three transition concerns. These points give structure to your Succession Readiness efforts and comprise the remaining chapters of this book:

Company

- **PLAN** – Your strategic plan should be right-sized for your organization and directionally accurate for the transition period and beyond. You know where you're headed this week and next month, but what about the future?

- **SUCCESSOR** – Your greatest impact now and in the future results from choosing the right successor and positioning that person to lead. Whom will you choose? And who makes up the team you engage around that person?

- **PRACTICALITIES** – Designating a successor means little without on-boarding that new leader into your role's real responsibilities. How will you coach your successor into these accountabilities before your exit?

Customers

- **RETENTION** – The customer-focused component of Maximum Momentum starts with identifying the business essential to retain in the transition. Which customer relationships are most at risk? Are there clients you need to fire before you move on?

- **CONNECTIONS** – Your successor needs more than casual introductions to established customers. How can you launch your successor as a capable and trustworthy partner worthy of continued business?

- **HANDOFF** – You've done your job when customers begin to look to your successor rather than you. What metrics prove the next leader is ready? When do you need to get out of the way?

Self

- **IDENTITY** – You might have vague wishes for your life after this business. What are your best options? How will you begin to test them? Will you stay connected to your organization financially and/or as an on-call expert?

- **RELATIONSHIPS** – Many exiting leaders face unanticipated challenges in clarifying expectations and building new habits with the people who matter most to them. How will you reinvest in those relationships starting now?

- **PURPOSE** – Executives who enjoy what comes next fill their days with more than activities. They ground themselves in purpose. How do your post-work plans position you to thrive beyond a few months?

If you neglect any component of the Maximum Momentum Triangle, you won't finish as well as you hope or achieve everything you worked hard for. You diminish your chances of going out on top.

The Maximum Momentum Triangle helps you identify unique needs across your transition. Assessing each component is essential to the best possible outcomes, and every situation starts with its own strengths and growth opportunities.

Personal Momentum

Let me be frank. People who run organizations well often don't plan well for life after work. They put everything firmly in place except their own plans.

As I said in chapter one, I'm writing this book for people who care about ensuring a powerful legacy. I've observed that many of these committed leaders neglect planning for their own future, at least beyond the financial. They toss out superficial answers like "I'm going to golf a lot" or assume questions like "What should I do?" will answer themselves. They won't.

This is so essential I'm saying it up front, even though tackling these questions will need to wait until the last chapters of this book. If leaders don't meet questions of their own future head on, they inadvertently set themselves up for disappointment. As an exiting leader, your satisfaction and peace of mind beyond the first few months of freedom deepens when you can do two things:

- **Look back with CONFIDENCE**—knowing you've done everything you can to set the organization up for success.

- **Look ahead with CLARITY**—discovering direction for your own version of a purposeful life after work.

That's the personal side of Maximum Momentum. If that sounds too squishy, it's your life to live. If you don't want to explore your future, you might as well keep doing what you're doing.

Seller Momentum

Many owners and their advisors conceive of maximum value narrowly, in purely financial terms. But a maximum dollar valuation and Maximum Momentum aren't mutually exclusive. It's not an either/or choice. Maximum Momentum is maximum financial value PLUS.

In the context of a sale, you'll need to meet countless financial and legal requirements, some well in advance of closing. Failing to promptly address those details puts you at risk of slowing a sale if not derailing it. Let your accountants and lawyers guide you through these decisions.

Experts in finance and law seldom see the whole picture. They share stories of how a protégé has derailed or added value. At the same time, they won't fully explore the people side of selling a business, because it's not their area of expertise. Yet undertaking a sale without strong attention to talent management is incomplete.

If your concern is selling for maximum dollar value, the business best practices embodied in Maximum Momentum help get you there. They address multiple underlying issues that contribute to peak financial valuation.

For example, will potential buyers see your people as assets? Do you have a thoroughly onboarded successor? Have you surrounded that person with a competent and complimentary team? Will potential buyers perceive your savvy talent practices and think, "Wow! I want those people. They're all keepers." Or will they say, "Wow! What a mess of liabilities. I've got at least three leaders I'd need to get rid of immediately."

It's like buying a move-in ready house vs. a fixer-upper. Your business will genuinely be healthier, buyers will perceive a well-run organization, and the value of your company will go up. If things are a mess, your asking price will appear unreasonable and you'll limit your buyer pool.

The Maximum Momentum Triangle guides you through another people issue often taken for granted during transition: customer retention. Your chosen successor must possess not only internal organizational competence but external credibility with customers, key influencers, and friends of the firm.

For example, when potential buyers study your company's valuation, they'll want to know details of existing contracts. But contracts ensure nothing more than temporary compliance. They don't address how customers feel about the transition nor do they guarantee customers won't flee the moment contracts expire. Most customers see leader transitions as opportunities to reexamine vendor relationships. Smart buyers probe the quality of a new leader's external connections, because established, authentic connections are where much long-term business value resides.

Maximum financial value derives from more than bare numbers. It's increased by perceived value and the story you can tell.

As seller, you plan to negotiate hard for maximum value on exit. You'll have a far more favorable dialog if you can convey not only current value but the direction of your organization. The buyer really wants to understand where you're going. Positive momentum makes you bigger than what you are right now. For lack of a better word, it makes you cool. When a buyer senses your momentum, you build confidence, lower perceived risk, and likely accelerate the sale cycle.

Exit Windows

You might have picked up this book looking for an instant solution. I can't alter the fact that the ideal timeframe for strategic executive succession is a window of three to five years.

If that sounds excessive, it coincides with the sales cycle most business valuation experts recommend. Accelerating the timeline is possible if you focus on core tasks:

- **THREE-YEAR WINDOW** – If you have a stretch of time to navigate your succession, you'll make your transition with peace of mind that you've made the most of the process—making sound decisions, setting the organization up for success, solidifying your legacy. If you're an owner, you'll also have the time it takes to fully maximize your valuation.

- **ONE-YEAR WINDOW** – If you're a year out, you can still accomplish some rapid schooling. Your core decisions should focus on choosing and developing the right successor, and ensuring that new leader's alignment with strategy. If you're an owner, adding the accounting and legal demands of a sale will keep you busy. But a year is enough for an exiting leader to make significant impact.

- **THREE- TO SIX-MONTH WINDOW** – Your goals during an accelerated departure depend on the situation. If an organization puts you on a path out, negotiate to participate on parts of the succession process where you most want a voice. If you're facing an urgent health issue, take care of yourself first. Decide who can best assume your responsibilities, usually your CFO or COO, until a successor lands. Put any remaining energy into determining specific qualifications of the organization's next leader. If you're an owner with an opportunity for a rapid sale, help your people clarify their roles under new ownership, and begin focusing on your own post-sale activities.

Momentum Multiplied

It can be wired into the DNA of leaders to go it alone at critical decision points, trusting their judgment to lead them the right way. If it's worked this far, why mess with success?

In decisions as big as a career finale, coaching a successor, and choosing new paths, you need more. Your informal networks offer a solid start. Touch base with friends who've exited leadership roles. Ask for honest answers to your toughest questions. You'll get starting points for thought and research. If a good friend succeeded one way, that might offer clues to you. If another struggled, take what you can from their experience.

Talking shop with friends, however, won't get you the complete solutions you need to go out on top. I encourage you to explore your needs and options through the rest of this book—looking first at your organization, then at your customers, and finally at yourself:

- **Company—chapters 3–5**

- **Customers— chapters 6–8**

- **Self—chapters 9–11**

Whatever transition you foresee, pursuing Maximum Momentum will improve your chances of getting where you want to go.

CHAPTER THREE

Company | Plan

Marcus was walking in the woods when he realized a switch had flipped inside him. In the past, he had fleeting thoughts of what it might look like to walk away from his business, but now a full press of thoughts and emotions alerted him that stepping out of active leadership merited more serious consideration.

The sensation accompanied yet another wave of grief over his parents passing two years before. The elderly couple was in good health and enjoying retirement when they died in an auto accident. Marcus never imagined the intense ache their absence would cause or that memories of his parents would grow more penetrating and profound by the day. He weighed two thoughts—first, that it was his responsibility to carry the torch for his generation, and second, that life can be shorter than we expect.

Often when Marcus drove home from the land where he and his dad had often walked and hunted, insights that seemed brilliant on the forest path lost their relevance. But today, Marcus mentally ticked through the years he might reasonably have left. Blocks of time fell into place. Life, death, health, continued work, grandbabies, aging, hobbies, exiting the business—they all had a place on his timeline.

Business-wise, Marcus knew he had put his organization on a path to ongoing success. He had taken over the commercial insurance firm from his father just before the Great Recession. No disrespect to his dad, but the company was stuck in the slow and safe world of the past. Marcus saw markets disappearing and faced a choice to adapt or die. His many dozens of employees had fallen through attrition from its pre-recession peak, but the company's volume and profits were significantly up.

The firm was full of committed employees who loved their work. Marcus was especially pleased with the younger employees he hired to focus on digital expansion. Their expertise brought efficiencies and increased customer satisfaction. Marcus had even grown a group of digital natives he billed out to other professional services firms.

Marcus had given up on the long-term strategic planning of his father's era. The marketplace was too volatile. Instead, he had refined an opportunistic methodology of dedicating resources to piloting new products, and testing markets and profitability. He rarely could predict exactly what would emerge, but this agility had given them a competitive advantage. Diverse offerings could come and go as markets grew and contracted, and entrepreneurial responsiveness would keep the company thriving.

If Marcus has a shortcoming as a leader, it's bringing people into his thinking. He quickly perceives the best course of action, but he's come to understand the delay others experience tracking the reasoning behind his decisions. As an exasperated employee told him, "I can't read your mind!" He's practicing slowing down, opening up about what he's thinking and why, and giving his people time to process.

Building Momentum

Picture the arc of your personal history of leading your company. Across that arc, you should always think and act to maximize organizational momentum.

There's never a time you can ignore best practices around talent identification and retention. You always need optimal systems for accounting or protecting intellectual property. Paying attention to customer care and other frontline services—that's just part of running a good business. This all should be the normal course of how you do business every day. It's how you set your company up for success. And grow your organization. And maximize value.

When you begin to approach your own potential exit—that window, ideally, three to five years out—it's time to double down on your intentionality. The energy you invest will spike, even if you're already working as hard as you know how. If you're moving so fast you lack time to reflect, now is the time to change that. Somehow.

As you consider transitioning out of a business, whatever shape that transition ultimately takes, you need time to build a good company or to make a good business even better. What creates great companies is disciplined effort over time around talent, processes, procedures—everything.

It's not like you can swoop in at the last minute, do quick fixes, apply duct tape and bubble gum, and just say, "Okay, this is a great company. It's ready for a leadership handoff." Successors want to step into an organization where everyone from the top leader to hourly team members can confidently say, "This is how we work all the time."

Maximum Momentum prior to a transition is simply good business with a refined focus. It isn't something you do on Tuesdays from 3 to 5pm. It integrates into your whole business, touching every decision you make.

If as a leader you haven't made the shift from working in the business to working on the business, the demands of succession will seem impossible to meet. Or if you haven't done good care and feeding of the business, you'll face the cost of lost opportunities as you spend time cleaning up messes. Those aren't reasons to stop thinking about transition. They're your rationale for starting early.

The better you run your business over time, the more readily you'll find time to manage the transition well and determine what comes next for you. You'll have energy to be intentional about each step that lies ahead.

Organizational Direction

Intentionality is the foundation of Succession Readiness. The Maximum Momentum Triangle starts with clarifying a plan for your organization, because all subsequent decisions cascade from that starting point.

Large companies undertake regular, systematic, intensive strategic planning. They fill in all the blanks and execute the plan.

I think they muck along more than they would admit.

That's probably not quite fair. It depends how detailed a strategic plan is. At its peak, General Electric pursued a strategy of looking for the top one or two organizations in a sector and buying them. The industry mattered little if the company was the market leader and the valuation good. GE didn't always know which companies it would buy or where the acquisitions were geographically located. What the strategic plan did was keep everyone moving in the same direction.

Understanding the point of planning is crucial. Most small- to mid-size companies don't engage in extensive future visioning. If your organization lacks a formal strategic plan, now is the time to spell out in broad terms where you're headed. In a moment, I'll outline uncomplicated steps to help you accomplish that. If you already possess a functioning strategy for your organization, I want you to understand where your plan fits into the transition process.

On the surface, executive transition is a simple problem to solve. You're going to leave. Someone else will take your place. The real trick is how that best happens.

You could choose a successor based on gut instinct. Or the ease of designating a lieutenant who happens to be within arm's reach. Achieving the best for everyone involved, however, requires you begin with an idea of where the organization is going—a PLAN. From there, you get specific about PRIORITIES. Once you've elevated tasks that matter most, you'll see more clearly what kind of people you need to move you toward your goals. Even if you have a successor in mind, I encourage you to step back and first consider your broader talent POOL before finalizing your choice of the PERSON who becomes your successor.

Here's what the process looks like:

PLAN ▷ PRIORITIES ▷ POOL ▷ PERSON

Building Succession Readiness starts with knowing where the organization is headed. Only then can you really identify the leader best able to take the organization into the future. And that person will appreciate your clarity around the actual mission at hand.

Directional Accuracy

Great leaders see the end from the beginning and lead followers into a better future.

If only the path of leadership were as smooth as that sounds. I've watched competent leaders stumble over predictable obstacles of executive transition:

- Exiting an organization—especially when it includes selling a business—disrupts routine. Most leaders don't make time to plot the future on normal days. How will you carve out time to reflect, brainstorm, and troubleshoot during a transition?

- Even the best successor has a limited capacity to absorb knowledge. Of all the hard-won lessons you've absorbed, which will you focus on passing along?

- Even the best organization has limited resilience. How will you prepare people for the changes ahead?

- Transitions raise deep emotional issues for leaders, including the difficulty of handing over control. When and how will you deal with your own stuff?

- Relationships are easily forgotten or mismanaged during seasons of stress. How will you divide your time among people clamoring for your attention?

- Determining what your days will look like after your exit is usually the hardest part of transition, the most taken for granted and therefore the most neglected. What will you do as an ex-leader?

- A leader's mind is often a black box of experience and instinct. How will you invite your successor and other leaders into your thinking?

The surest way to surmount these obstacles is to project a clear path forward for your organization, a plan that maintains your focus and guides you as you drive toward your desired end.

Succession Readiness doesn't require you to throw away the planning process that got you this far. For most small- to mid-size businesses, the right-sized strategic plan is primarily about being directionally accurate.

Developing a minutely-detailed vision of the future when that's not your gift will derail you. Or taking months to develop a comprehensive strategic plan will probably kill you long before you put it into action. The real value of strategic planning is getting people talking about the future and generating possibilities.

Your right-sized plan is likely more general than you might expect. You want to have conversations around overarching questions:

- In the most basic terms, what makes our organization successful?

- What challenges are we facing?

- What opportunities are we neglecting?

- What are we doing that deviates from our core competencies and takes us off track?

- What key areas do we need to focus on during the next three years to be successful?

Out of those conversations should come a basic plan that is directionally accurate—headlined by a simple statement of who you are and where you are headed: "We're entrepreneurial and agile." "We want to go deeper, not broader." "We need to aggressively counter strong competition." "We grow through acquisitions." "We need to consolidate our gains." Those are directionally accurate statements. They don't describe all the details. But they're enough to define where you're headed.

For example, consider a company that grows through acquisitions. Looking back on their history, that's repeatedly been the source of their best growth and profitability. More specifically, they know they specialize in growth through geographic expansion into new markets, buying similar companies and replicating their lean business model. They're always actively searching and shopping for businesses to buy, but they never know where opportunities will emerge. As a mid-size company, that plan is enough to keep them directionally accurate. Acting outside that plan could be a major misstep.

The above questions are relevant anytime you need to think broadly about your organizational plan. As you craft a directionally-accurate plan during succession, the additional questions you need to answer sound like this:

- How could my departure impact the overall direction of the business?

- What opportunities exist to stop doing things because of a leadership transition?

- How aggressively should we plan to grow through a transition—or should we pull back and maintain?

- What obvious weakness do we need to address for the organization to be ready for my eventual departure?

- (For owners) What multiple do I want to achieve in a sale? What concrete changes must happen to get maximum financial value?

Early in your exit planning, you'll want to keep these transition conversations within your trusted circle of advisors. In a moment we'll get to thoughts on who can contribute to your planning.

Organizational Resilence

Strategy isn't everything. When organizations experience stress, what sustains them is strong culture.

As the Great Recession unfolded, I watched company after company begin to struggle, including those among my clients. You might be surprised by which organizations survived. It wasn't necessarily businesses with the best strategies or largest bank accounts. Many of those companies stumbled. Some no longer exist. Those that survived had a people-focused culture. They probably didn't make much money during the recession, but they made it through reasonably intact.

It's true that the financial health of some companies that went under was just a façade. Being overleveraged put them at risk. But the trait shared by companies that struggled the most was that their people worked for the money, not the mission. When paychecks suffered, people asked, "Why am I here?" Employee disengagement and loss of talent accelerated business decline. A lack of shared purpose made it easy to leave.

Many circumstances can make a company vulnerable, but a strong culture empowers people to ride it out together.

A transition shouldn't rock your organization to the extent of a global economic contraction, but the principle remains the same. During the stress of leadership change, a strong culture will sustain the organization.

As you consider putting your organization through a leadership transition, don't neglect this need to build resilience.

The markers of strong culture include the following:

- Respectful leadership

- Competence across the top

- Sound processes for making decisions

- Reasonable transparency

- Customer-service culture, internally and externally

- Acting in line with organizational values, with follow-through that puts words into practice

You can incorporate the following culture-building questions into your planning conversations:

- What features of our culture attract and retain the best people?

- What cultural strengths have helped us surmount previous challenges?

- Where do we fall short on the markers of strong culture?

Strong habits around culture help your organization bridge the stresses as you walk out and the next leader walks in. If you don't have culture-building habits in place, make them a key part of your overall plan.

Identifying Priorities

Priorities are the practical actions that derive from a directionally accurate plan. If you know where you're going, what steps will get you there?

Obviously, you want to make choices that, within the limits of your resources, move you furthest and fastest toward your goals. So what priorities emerge from your planning?

What to do is only half the problem. In the context of Succession Readiness, who will help you is the other half.

In the normal life of your organization, you know who to tap to make things happen. Unless you're a sole business owner with sole control of every decision, however, you answer to others, whether an informal family council or a board exercising oversight of a private business, publicly traded company, or non-profit entity. Perhaps a subset of that group deals with succession issues.

Board involvement in your decision-making around succession always hinges on the function and oversight level of the board—do they drive the process or watch over it? The choice of when and how you let the board into your thinking depends on your own comfort level as well as board expectations. Consulting the board chair when you have reasonable certainty you want to move on is a likely first step.

Whether or not you answer to a board, in the short-term, your usual team of internal leaders won't likely provide much help on anything having to do with your transition. First, you want to retain power to make decisions based on Maximum Momentum—what's best for the company, its customers, and your own future, not be driven by others' personal agendas. Second, people who work for you aren't interested in riding your rollercoaster of thoughts and emotions as you consider your departure—their job, after all, is to do their job. When it does come time to enlist internal help, your CFO or HR leader might be the first person you turn to.

In the context of turning your plan into priorities, it's often the triumvirate of outside accountant, lawyer, and talent management expert who can give the most relevant guidance.

I've already referred to these financial, legal, and talent professionals as your close, trusted advisors. If you combine their perspectives, you get a good picture of what's entailed in exiting a business. Each point of view is essential if you're an owner planning to sell. And these experts are often your best help in setting priorities.

- **An accountant** will audit your finances, ensuring your books are in order and policies and practices are in place, as well as certifying a history of good practices over time, not just a last-minute cleanup of your books. CPA involvement isn't just for succession. It's a best practice always, and in the case of a sale, it ultimately ensures no surprises for a buyer.

- **A lawyer** will audit all things legal, examining items including intellectual property and the necessity of protections like trademarks and patents, as well as terms of employee and vendor contracts and more. You should always have a lawyer safeguarding your legal exposure.

- **A talent management expert** will audit your people, delving into leadership and culture, coaching people for the next level, and identifying the successor. Bringing in a talent advisor early in your Succession Readiness process will help you figure out your path, prepare the senior leadership team, and drive the issues discovered in the audit.

These advisors will each give you a checklist for now and into the future. They will set a significant number of your priorities, and generally those items will take time to fix. It's why you're best served by a longer period of three to five years to achieve Succession Readiness.

A CPA, for example, might find a serious problem with inventory, a lot of liability for a future owner to take on. And they're going to dig into the organization and uncover strengths and weaknesses. Lawyers and talent management advisors do the same.

You can do an audit with an attorney for best practices without beginning transition discussions. You'll need their involvement for a sale, but conversations heavy on legalese can get expensive quickly.

Ultimately, you control whom you involve in your planning and prioritizing. Think in terms of concentric circles. You know your situation best, so map this out. Draw a bullseye with you in the center. As you move outward, how will you expand the circles? Be thoughtful about who you bring into your deliberations—and when.

Voice of the Buyer

If you're an owner looking to sell or a leader of an organization likely to be acquired, you might hear potential buyers wanting to insert themselves into your organizational plan.

Considering those points of view might not sit well with you. You might already feel like your exit is letting others dictate what happens with your business. You can decide, however, to control what you can about choosing a buyer. There's a world of difference between selling to

- A team member you've prepared as your successor

- An association of employees

- An industry associate who aligns with your mission

- A buyer who wants a portion of your business but not all

- A hands-off investor in your industry with a philosophy of buy-hold-grow

- A transactional investor looking to cut costs, sell prime assets, and hold a fire sale of what's left

Again, within the limits of your control, you can decide now who you want to sell to. Questions to consider include:

- What kind of buyer am I looking for?

- How much does it matter that a buyer aligns with my values?

- How will I vet a buyer's values alignment?

- Who will I prefer not to sell to?

- Who will I never sell to?

The core question is how your preferred buyer might shape or remake your overall organizational plan. How might your direction change? What priorities will you tweak, add, or subtract?

Next Steps

There's no one-size-fits-all list of the plan and priorities that will prepare your organization for succession. The goals, permutations, contingencies, and what-ifs are countless. But when you possess a directionally accurate plan with priority action items, you'll be ready to move to the next step of Maximum Momentum, ensuring you find the right people to lead your organization into the future.

CHAPTER FOUR

Company | Successor

When Dave excused himself from dessert to take a call, his wife, Becky, leaned in with a question for the younger couple across the table of a Texas steakhouse. "When are you going to buy this business?"

Over the course of most of his adult life, Dave had built his service company into an upper-Midwest powerhouse. He had talked about selling for years, and Becky was done with talk. They were in their 70s, and she had begun asking whose name would be etched on the gravestone next to his—the company's or her own.

Jason and Kimberly were obvious potential buyers. The couple and business duo led a smaller yet similarly dominant company in the Southwest, and right from the start they felt like family. Dave called them their "long-lost boot-wearing kinfolk." A trade show created a reason for the couples to get together, and their dinner was an enjoyable third or fourth round of catching up, trading industry gossip, and gaining trust. Becky, however, feared the evening would once again end with nothing more than friendly words about staying in touch.

When Dave returned from his call and Kimberly announced that Becky had just "popped the question," Becky turned to her husband and asked, "Are you going to do this—or not?"

Dave wasn't prepared to let go of his company on the spot, but he also wasn't ready to dismiss his younger counterparts. Becky's question catalyzed serious conversations, and less than a year later, the deal was done.

Conversation Killers

If you care about the organization you lead, then it matters that you find your match with the person who will succeed you. Whether your successor is a new owner, an outside hire, or an internal protégé, if you want to ensure your legacy, a lot of courtship needs to transpire.

Many leaders kill conversations with potential successors even before they start, missteps that look a lot like dating disasters. Even as you rate others, they rate you. They might sense the relationship just isn't clicking. Or they see something in you or your organization that makes them run the other way. Some examples:

Lack of Commitment

Dave enjoyed his conversations with Jason and Kimberly, not to mention the attention and admiration they showered on him, but he stalled when it came time for commitment. Leaders who are considering exiting frequently act out this approach-avoid, hot-cold, on-off, start-stop dynamic, often for years. The best potential successors won't wait forever.

Business Baggage

Only turnaround specialists enjoy cleaning up messes. Business flaws and failings scare people away in a hurry. People looking at a leadership role or at buying your organization will decide some issues are too big to deal with.

Desperation

If you're on life support in a declining industry or not keeping up with innovations in your market, your organization won't be viable without a major intervention. Outsiders suspect you're still on the market for good reason, and the courtship will quickly fade.

Playing Hard To Get

For owners, the most common conversation stopper is overvaluing the business, asking for an outrageous multiple. If the industry standard, for example, is a multiple of five, they want 12. That shortsighted move could be naiveté or ego or both.

Of course, sellers always believe their business is worth more, and buyers always deem it worth less. If you're an owner, beware of filtering your asking price through your emotions. Your investment of sweat and tears can cause you to inflate the price unrealistically, and you'll scare off buyers who just want to see your P&L and draw their own conclusions about a reasonable offer.

Culture Shock

Suppose a leader with a team-based approach tries to step into a top-down company. That new leader will find it nearly impossible to overcome the existing culture. The employees are acclimated to an environment of dependence, and a new collaborative approach won't automatically empower them to think and act on their own. The risk of a culture disaster is high, and the leadership patterns so different it's just not worth it.

Altering your behavior can ward off some of these conversation killers. Others require addressing core characteristics of your organization. Then you'll attract the quality potential successors you seek, strengthen your ability to sustain conversations, and close the deal.

Start with Values

There are many reasons you might rule potential successors in or out. One should outweigh the rest. If a new leader doesn't align with your core values, move on. The transition will be painful and the likelihood of positive outcomes low.

Every organization struggles to adapt during leadership transitions. It's not just that people dislike change or don't want to adjust to differing leadership styles. If the variations are minor, the company will probably be okay. But if a new leader doesn't match with established values, you're asking for trouble.

Sometimes a leader needs to transition out of a business suddenly for health or other urgent reasons. It's understandable if that leader takes the first successor who comes along. But in every other situation, there's no excuse for not looking for a values match. If you're serious about your legacy, start there. Make values alignment your first cut for qualifying potential successors.

Conversations about values often happen naturally early in a succession process. You're on the alert for potential replacements, whether potential buyers, external leaders, or internal candidates. Early conversations usually focus on getting know each other's backgrounds, swapping tales of leadership wins and losses, and debating strategy. If you're paying attention at all, you begin to understand what make people tick—motivations, goals, pains, dreams—all of which communicate values. You can further uncover values with questions like

- What do you consider your signature accomplishments?

- Who has shaped your leadership style and skills?

- When as a leader have you most struggled?

- If you could go back and remake your career path, what would you do differently?

- What goals do you still want to achieve?

If your values align, it's easy to picture that person partnering with you and eventually assuming your leadership role. That's great. When core values are aligned, everyone involved has a happier transition.

But there's a catch.

Succeed and Surpass

Many leaders make the mistake of choosing a successor based primarily on personal comfort with a candidate. But the right match must also meet rigorous competence standards specific to your needs. Pick an individual capable not only of succeeding you but surpassing you.

Leaders often zero in on compatibility questions like

- Do we trust each other?

- Is there chemistry in our working relationship?

- Is this person's background and expertise like mine?

Those answers matter. But your successor also needs the capacity to lead the organization, coming on board with the plans and priorities you've identified. Deciding if an individual makes that cut requires evaluating core competencies of leadership success. Does the person have

- business judgment?

- financial acumen?

- leadership skills?

If the company is closely held, it's more likely hiring decisions will be biased toward personal factors.

The danger of choosing a successor because of personal fit is seeing a candidate's best qualities while overlooking that person's dark side. For example, a CEO might experience a potential internal successor as a high-trust, high-competence leader. The rest of the organization sees anything but that. They don't trust this person. They watch him throw others under the bus to cover his own shortcomings. When colleagues protest, the CEO says, "You don't understand him. You don't see his talents." That's common.

Another major mistake is choosing a successor for the past instead of the future. Your best pick is an individual who won't just replicate your work but extend it—who won't just replace you but build on what you've done.

It's possible to filter out your own biases, blind spots, even favoritism through robust talent management.

Talent Management Mindset

Talent Management is a technical business discipline that ensures you hire, develop, and retain people with the cultural fit and capabilities they need for success. A Talent Management Mindset powers the rigorous selection necessary to create Maximum Momentum.

At a basic level, a succession plan is always necessary—an outline of who will step up in the unfortunate event that one day you get hit by a bus. Leaders who are highly disciplined around product development, finances, customer orientation, and every other component of business success often don't think about "What happens if...."

In the growth of every organization, a necessary evolution should take place:

- At the start, every organization is **leader-centered.**

- Good leaders get out of their own way and make the organization **team-centered.**

- Great leaders create **talent-centered** organizations, with a long-term people plan driving development across the enterprise.

Put simply, in the rhythm of everyday business, a Talent Management Mindset means you're always thinking about

- Who does what?

- What should each person in our organization do next?

- Which individuals are moving in, up, across, down, or out?

This especially applies to the next CEO and the next one after that. If you're undertaking your organization's first CEO succession, everyone's outlook must change. Change at the top is the new normal. As the future unfolds, there will again be CEO transitions. How often should you have succession discussions? Who should be involved? How can you normalize the process and plan for change?

A Talent Management Mindset means recognizing the value of your people and developing individuals and teams to their greatest potential. You see your organization through the lens of talent.

Some leaders see everything through a financial lens. Or an operational lens. Some say they value their people but do little to demonstrate that concern. For example, they regard employee development as a cost, not an investment.

A Talent Management Mindset means seeing every step in the employee lifecycle—from entry to exit, from recruiting, hiring, and onboarding to day-in-day-out work—as a growth opportunity. It means committing to developing individuals throughout their time in your organization.

If you believe people matter to your business, you see everything differently:

- What culture do we want to create?

- Whom do we want to attract?

- How do we engage and retain the best employees?

- How do we show people respect?

- How do we respond to toxic influences?

- How do we best serve our customers?

Picture the salesperson who bullies coworkers yet makes a pile of money. An organization with a profit-driven mindset puts that person on a pedestal. If you truly value talent across your organization, that's not good enough.

Some leaders think this people-focus is baloney. The cynical part of me says, "We'll see you in bankruptcy court."

If you don't want to invest in talent management, you can make that choice. But you'll be hard-pressed to recruit and retain talent without a people-centric mindset. You'll lose millennials, who realize you won't invest in their career. You'll never create the renowned culture that even customers want to be a part of because all your employees are on Glassdoor griping about the jerk at the top. In the social media world, there are no secrets.

It's tough to build an organization and prosper without paying attention to your people. Maximum Momentum depends on it.

The Pool

Creating Maximum Momentum for your organization in preparation for your transition requires not just choosing the right successor but preparing the senior management team. Addressing the entire team builds viability and value.

Even if you have a successor in mind, I want to invite you to step back and think about larger talent issues. You might be thinking, "We have our plan and priorities in place. Who is the right **person**?" I want you to first consider, "With our plan and priorities in place, who are our best **people**?

Recall this process flow from chapter three:

PLAN ▸ **PRIORITIES** ▸ **POOL** ▸ **PERSON**

From a talent management perspective, it's preferable to evaluate the people at the top of your organization and then narrow to a possible successor than to select the successor and assemble a team to surround that person.

Sometimes a successor is obvious. But more often than not, identifying a successor early means shortcutting rigorous evaluation. You're comfortable with someone and that individual knows the business. But can that person really lead?

Leaders are notorious for not being able to evaluate their own replacement. They pick badly.

Moreover, if you line up your successor and never look broadly at the pool, it's easy to end up with a big hitter but no bench. You forget about the rest of the team. Are they competent and qualified? Are they worthy of a new leader's trust? Will they stay?

Given adequate time pre-transition, a talent management advisor can help you assess your team's strengths and weaknesses, coach the team to greater cohesiveness, or prepare them for change.

By evaluating the whole leadership team and creating an appropriate development plan for everyone, each individual will do better. Through assessments, feedback, coaching, and development activities, the whole team raises its game. Evaluating your team may include removing and replacing people who aren't performing well.

Be careful about designating one person as the savior who will assume leadership of your organization, figure out a team, and make everything fine. For a successful transition and, if you're an owner, a maximum value sale, you need high-performing upper management. Start with the right people in the right places. Who earns a place on your top team? Why? Once you answer those questions, then you can better discern who might emerge as successor.

Identifying Successor Competencies

Nothing drives an organization like having the right people in the right places empowered to achieve optimal results. As your organization moves forward, those results are determined more than anything else by your choice of successor.

You're not looking for an easy choice, a premature choice, or a pressured choice. You want to make the Maximum Momentum choice that will achieve the best for your company, your customers, and even your own future.

I believe you need the input of a talent management advisor to get there. That person brings an outside voice that says, "Let's take stock. Let's get some objective data." You get the facts you need for deliberate decision-making, an evidence-based approach that doesn't leave you guessing. Just like an accountant helps with money issues and a lawyer with legal concerns, a talent management expert helps on people issues. This advisor will help you break down your biases, make legally-defensible decisions, and increase your likelihood of a successful transition.

Well-grounded successor decisions begin with identifying leadership needs that emerge from your plan and priorities, not with tailoring a job description to fit a favored candidate. While each talent management advisor brings a unique approach to this task, I'll spell out what this process looks like in my practice at Corporate Psychologists.

Context

When we assist an organization approaching key leader succession, we start by drawing out a thorough understanding of the organization's overall plan along with details of the transition. What's the business strategy? What's needed most—continuity, innovation, turnaround, growth, cost cutting, defensive measures? It goes back to directional accuracy. Where are you now—and where are you headed? And what's the timeline?

Competencies

With an understanding of the business context, we help the organization determine the competencies the leader needs to deliver results— the right mix of knowledge, experience, and skills. We develop a model to evaluate how candidates

- Think strategically

- Build talent

- Foster collaboration

- Leverage change

- Drive results

Those high-level themes encompass multiple competencies. The analysis they inform isn't a black box. Each competency is grounded in observable behaviors.

For high-stakes succession decisions, we take candidates through comprehensive leadership assessments that include interviews, personality inventories, cognitive testing, and work simulations. Some elements measure candidates against benchmarks. Other components don't have right answers. But some answers are better than others, and responses indicate a candidate's priorities.

We provide assessments and feedback in three categories:

Leadership Readiness

Evaluation of a candidate's *current* readiness for a *specific* role. Crucial for succession hiring and promotion decisions. Results indicate:

- **Ready now**—likely to be successful

- **Ready now with developmental support**—likely to be successful, but will need help with one or more development areas

- **Not ready**—unlikely to be successful without significant development = do not recommend

Leadership Potential

Insights into a candidate's long-term leadership potential. Useful for successor onboarding and development. Best interpreted with other information about an individual, including performance record. Results indicate:

- **Strength**—likely to be a long-term strength

- **Capable**—likely to be a strength if intentionally developed, but may become a need if neglected

- **Need**—likely to present long-term challenges

Leadership Derailers

Evidence of leadership derailment risks. Guides onboarding, development, and coaching. Results indicate:

- **Low risk**—unlikely to be a problem

- **Medium risk**—may be a problem; monitor

- **High risk**—likely to be a problem without development

A seasoned talent management advisor will use similar assessments and the resulting data to make recommendations and help guide your decisions.

Choosing Your Successor

Once you establish competencies based on your organizational plan and priorities, you can begin assessing candidates. And with that data in hand, you can answer your pressing questions: Who emerges at the top? Do you have an internal successor? Do you need to look outside? If you're an owner looking to sell, how do potential buyers measure up?

Rigorous leadership assessments against role-specific competencies might identify a successor ready to lead right now. Or someone who can be developed to step up. Or you might find no one you've evaluated thus far is ready to succeed you now or in the future.

Ready Successor

If you have a potential successor who is largely prepared for the role, now is the time for dialog. What is that person's interest level? Will succession entail a financial stake in the company or buying it outright? What does that individual need to know to reach a decision?

Never initiate conversations without knowing how to bring them to clear conclusions. For example, over several years, the CEO of a family-owned business had discussed succession possibilities with several internal leaders. When he died unexpectedly, oversight of the business fell to family members that previously had minimal involvement. Several employees came forward, each asserting a claim to be the late CEO's handpicked successor, and everyone wound up in court.

Successor Needing Development

Can you identify a successor who could be ready for the job if given adequate development? Or would no amount of effort be enough to qualify that person for your role?

Now is the time to leverage assessment feedback to detail development needs and create a timeline for growth. We'll cover the pragmatic concerns of onboarding any new leader in depth in chapter five.

In addition to building knowledge, experience, and skills, internal successors often need preparation for the upcoming psycho-social upheaval. Many don't feel ready for the responsibility. Most don't anticipate the shock of being alone at the top. If you've evaluated your entire leadership pool, you can discern who is present to support the new leader or who might leave if they aren't chosen to lead.

Going Outside

Considering outside candidates enables you to discover new talent and further measure your internal people. If you're starting from scratch in getting to know external candidates, it's all the more important to leverage your competency model and assessments to size up possibilities. You'll likely want to engage an external search firm to bridge the gap between you and qualified successors.

If you're an owner anticipating selling to an outside buyer, identifying a successor isn't an exercise in futility. Putting a strong leadership team in place is still your prime opportunity to safeguard your legacy and ensure the organization can withstand the challenges of transition. Talk with your talent management advisor about additional competencies your successor might need as well as ways to communicate risk and reward to leaders facing the likelihood of a sale.

Again, no decision is more consequential to your organization than your choice of successor. You should reach that decision based on more than personal fit or gut instinct. Work with your talent management advisor to define the competencies most needed in your situation, assess candidates thoroughly, and leverage all sources of information as you decide.

What Comes Next

Choosing a successor is just the first step in that new leader's journey. For the next phase of transition, you need to find a way to lead in tandem, guiding your successor into the most essential parts of what you know.

Ensuring a business thrives into the future requires you facilitate that person's onboarding to the greatest extent the situation allows. Setting that person up for success is your next step toward Maximum Momentum.

CHAPTER FIVE

Company|
Practicalities

From the moment Shelby first stepped to the microphone at an annual gala celebrating the non-profit he founded, Fred knew he had discovered his successor. The crowd hung on Shelby's stories of the wins and heartaches of clients they served. By the end, many listeners were wiping away tears.

In the years since, Shelby rose from field staff to Vice President of Operations, overseeing a dozen sites staffed by more than a hundred employees and many hundreds of volunteers. For nearly a year, she has done double-duty, covering her role plus fundraising oversight, with the result that contributions are higher than ever.

When the organization marked its 25th anniversary, Fred began discussing a five-year exit strategy with his board. He remained enthusiastic about the mission and had no intention of ever walking away completely, and the board agreed he would retain the title of Founder and Executive Director Emeritus, which came with a modest stipend and a board seat.

The group's charter required an open and transparent succession process, and Shelby was one of several candidates in a tough field. Interviews, assessments, and a board vote confirmed what Fred saw years earlier. Shelby was the right person for the job.

While Fred was overjoyed for Shelby, once the succession decision was made, he sensed unexpected tension. He felt pressure to step down sooner than planned, possibly even to give up his board seat. Shelby wanted to take away everything he had built, and he was unprepared for a lesser role.

After years of putting all his hopes for the organization's future on Shelby, Fred felt she had betrayed his trust. She was loudly asserting her vision and letting it be known she didn't appreciate him questioning her initiatives.

In Shelby's view, Fred was no longer capable of leading, and she was campaigning for him to go.

It all felt like a coup.

Succession Stressors

Executive succession is rife with risks, some expected, some not.

Your successor, for instance, faces a greater than 50-50 chance of failure, and lack of preparation is at the heart of the problem:

- Citing a 10-year study that says that 61% of executives reported being unprepared for the strategic challenges of senior leadership, author Ron Carruci says, "It's no surprise, then, that 50%–60% of executives fail within the first 18 months of being promoted or hired." He adds, "Appointing that many unprepared leaders into roles directly responsible for crafting and executing strategy only fuels the risk of executional failure."[1]

- Noting that 50-70% of executives fail within the first 18 months of promotion into an executive role, whether coming from within the organization or from outside, the Corporate Executive Board reports that of those who fail, about 3% "fail spectacularly" while nearly 50% "quietly struggle."[2]

If your successor will face difficulties—and that's guaranteed—you also will endure strains. Many departing CEOs describe transition as an ugly, painful time.

If you're truly eager to choose a successor and exit, happy results can follow. But if you're hesitant to leave when others sense your best days are over, there's a good chance you'll feel pressure from underneath to get out. Your up-and-comers believe they know what's best for the organization, an attitude that often comes with a sense of entitlement that they deserve the recognition and rewards of being the next leader.

If you like being in charge and don't want to give up your role, be honest with yourself. If you can't let go, own that. Consult with your talent management advisor before making major decisions, leveraging that sounding board to fully explore repercussions. And look at your real reasons for backpedaling. Hesitation often stems from not knowing what your life holds after your exit. Chapters 9–11 of this book will help you map your next steps.

You can only stall so long before the system breaks. Potential internal successors want a clear path to the top, and the impatient will leave. Even a signed and sealed replacement can bolt, creating a catastrophic leadership gap that sets back succession by years and cuts off your exit for a long time to come. Uncertainty eventually drives out other employees. For the moment, most will stay head-down and watch the drama unfold. But the distraction inevitably causes a productivity decline, and your people will polish their resumes just in case.

Succession Management

Once you've identified a successor, your job is to make room for that person to lead, preparing that individual for future success.

Onboarding a successor is a bittersweet handover of power. You let go of your organization in whole or piece by piece, and your replacement picks up those accountabilities. What the process looks like varies by setting, but the objective is for the new leader to grapple with all the pragmatic components of your role.

The usual onboarding tips are relevant to your new leader:

- Determine priorities

- Establish accountabilities

- Secure early wins

- Communicate. Communicate. Communicate.

Those tips, however, don't clearly define your part. To the extent you can exert control moving forward, you function as succession manager. You might need to educate stakeholders about this role and advocate for your involvement.

For example, in board-driven environments, everything depends on how the board sees its role. Passive boards expect the top executive to lead. Operational boards want in on the details. Strategic boards want to set direction. Each board type approaches succession differently but identifying and hiring the organization's top leader is one of a board's primary responsibilities.

Under a board, you won't have the final decision regarding who succeeds you. But you usually have power to prepare your leadership team to transition well. If you have influence left to spend, use it to equip and empower the next leader. You're in a unique position to onboard that individual to ensure the organization's well-being when you're no longer around.

The Successor Cycle

From the first whispers of your departure, your role begins to undergo a transformation. As you transition, you move along a continuum from powerful leader to influential advisor, from boss to coach.

Depending on your circumstances, your power to command others will fade, slowly or in an instant. What continues is your capacity to coach.

It easy to coach for what you've already done. More difficult is to coach for what your successor will need to do. But your goal is to coach the new leader for the future—for what the business will be rather than what the business has been.

The Successor Cycle is the ongoing process of aligning values, sharing knowledge, transferring responsibility, and coaching performance. Just when you think you're done, the process restarts. Shifting responsibilities to your successor, for example, brings opportunities to coach. Coaching discussions inevitably circle back to aligning values. And the cycle goes on.

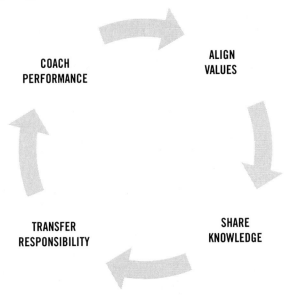

COACH PERFORMANCE

ALIGN VALUES

TRANSFER RESPONSIBILITY

SHARE KNOWLEDGE

THE SUCCESSOR CYCLE

From your first conversations with a potential successor, you've been ensuring values alignment. By swapping war stories or working together, you've shared knowledge. You can easily get stuck and progress no further than enjoying all the ways you agree with each other and sharing favorite tales.

Transferring responsibility is what matters now. It's where the hard work happens.

Transferring Responsibility

Your task is to bring your successor into the normal course of business, the full breadth and depth of your job. Some details to explore:

- What fills up your days?

- What keeps you awake at night?

- How many activities, interactions, relationships, and accountabilities of your role can you list, explain, and hand off?

- Which activities are essential? Which are not? Why?

- What plans and priorities are already in motion?

- How do you work with your leadership team?

- Where do you reach down and direct lower levels of the organization?

- What outlier situations might the new leader encounter?

- Where are the organizational skeletons? Quicksand? Landmines?

- What leadership competencies are most important to your job?

- If you went away tomorrow, what would you want your successor to know? Be able to solve? Be able to overcome?

Most simply, you're inviting your successor to run the business while you're still around to help.

You don't simply transfer responsibility. You also coach performance.

One of the biggest obstacles you might face in onboarding is letting your successor inside your head. The new leader needs to look through your eyes and walk in your shoes. You might need to articulate principles and practices you've never had to make explicit. In the past, you could get away with giving directions without explanations. When you're moving at the speed of business, that feels expedient. In onboarding a successor, that approach is completely inadequate. Your successor needs to understand not only **what** you do—or even **how**—but **why**.

One CEO was so intuitive about his business, he struggled to put things into words. He knew what to do, executed, and expected others to follow his lead. His habit of uttering few words frustrated his successor, an internal protégé. By investing time listening and talking, they could work it through. That's a helpful takeaway. Pause. Talk. Debate. Conclude.

As you transfer responsibility, your starting points are the details of your role and the practices you've used to successfully onboard employees in the past. But don't get lost in minutiae. At a high level, what does your successor need to accomplish?

Top leaders have duties that fall primarily to them, and the organization succeeds or fails based on how well the leader executes these key tasks. While others contribute to these five ends, final responsibility lands on your desk.

Only the CEO can...

- **SET DIRECTION.** What methodology do you use to determine organizational direction? Who do you involve or exclude in planning? Why? What forward-looking initiative can your successor take up immediately?

- **WIN FOLLOWERS.** What internal and external stakeholders are essential to success? Who will resist change? How will you connect the new leader throughout the organization?

- **ALLOCATE RESOURCES.** How do you effectively distribute resources between competing demands? How will supply and demand rise or fall in the future? What enterprise-wide resource decisions can your successor make now?

- **OWN PROBLEMS.** How do you speak to and for the organization? What vocabulary do you use to admit problems in public and in private? How can your successor avoid your missteps and build on your best habits?

- **PRESS ON.** How do you keep going when you feel alone at the top? How do you maintain perspective and vision? What organizational challenges need immediate attention? How will you phase out so your successor can take charge?

What other high-level themes would you add for your setting? What responsibilities fall squarely if not solely on you?

Formalizing Transition

Managing succession is like teaching someone to drive. You don't hand over the keys and walk away. But there comes a time when you must exit the vehicle and trust your student to drive alone. Your continued presence is counterproductive to learning and independence.

The timeframe you overlap with your replacement varies tremendously by situation, from years of grooming an internal successor to little or no time in some sales situations. Often the timeline is up to you, whether you leave suddenly, drift away, or intentionally stage your way out.

In the case of a sale, my observations are that an owner should limit their stay to no more than six months after closing. A longer period feels like you have forever to work things out, and you'll put off tasks you ought to complete. Allow too much time and you'll feel like a lame duck with no reason to show up at work. That six-month timeframe forces you and your successor to focus. At the end point, it's best to rip off the Band-Aid and be done. You do everything you can to help with the transition, then get out of the way.

It's incredibly unproductive to just let a transition happen and feel your way through as you go. Whatever your situation, put key points in a written transition plan, complete with timeline.

The components of a comprehensive leadership transition plan include

- Accountabilities to transfer

- Relationships to hand off

- Metrics or other markers to demonstrate progress

- Successor development points and agreement to a coaching plan

- Scheduled meetings between you and your successor

- Organizational communication plans

- Timeline of stages and milestones, including your final date on the job

Regular meetings will keep the transition on track, but it's up to you and your successor to determine the frequency of your interactions. Who runs the meetings will be a significant marker of the progress of your transition. A pattern of you or your successor postponing or cancelling these meetings isn't a good sign. Getting back on track should be a point of conversation, intentionality, and mutual accountability.

Communicating Change

By the point you're timelining succession steps, many in your organization need to know what lies ahead. If you've kept your trusted circle small, you need to widen the circle.

Employees are often the last to know about changes at the top, and they're usually caught by surprise. Of course, if there's an internal succession with an heir apparent, employees will snoop it out, and the transition might be the worst kept secret in the company. In the case of an outside buyer, employees wonder about strangers walking around. Rumors start, but most people are still surprised when something happens. Communication with the employees—messaging, methods, timing—are crucial.

Many transitioning leaders give ample time to details like finances and knowledge transfer. Some spend so much time on those pieces they forget about people. In one instance, the arrival of new ownership was announced with a memo tacked to the breakroom wall. A day or two later, someone brought a box of donuts. That was it for information and assimilation.

What is your plan for disseminating information and managing change? How can you act with intention and improve on even your best communication efforts in the past?

Coaching Performance

The handoff of organizational leadership creates an unusual and uncomfortable dynamic. From the moment others learn of your departure, your power begins to fade. As you transfer responsibilities to your successor and provide necessary feedback, you assume the role of coach.

Employees respond to the tone of your voice, a stance, the raise of an eyebrow. As your reign ends, a new way of getting things done can take its place. You shift from boss to coach.

BOSS	COACH
Hierarchy	Partnership
Manage	Collaborate
Direct	Advise

BOSS	COACH
Tell	Ask
Require	Request
Command	Suggest

Effective leaders always adapt their leadership style to fit varying situations, and you've no doubt effectively slipped into coaching mode all along. That adaptation was partial, temporary, and reversible. This isn't that. For the moment, you might retain full control. But transition puts you on a different trajectory.

Your movement from command to influence is inevitable, but you're not the only person in the succession process who must adapt. Coaches begin by evaluating a client's willingness to engage in the coaching process, their "coachability." Your successor must allow you to coach for the role you hand off. You might also choose to coach for the development gaps and potential derailers identified in assessments, or you might prefer to bring in outside expertise.

Building a formal coaching plan into your transition is a talent management best practice. Just as important is the conversation that informs the plan. You need to have what millennials call a "DTR" conversation with your successor—determine the relationship. What's the nature of the relationship between you and your successor today? How does it change at key stages of the transition? How about after you exit? Are you able to make the change from boss to coach? Is your successor agreeable to coaching?

If you're unwilling to shift to coach mode, you'll need to get out of the way sooner rather than later. If your primary style of interacting with your successor is barking commands, you'll need to designate someone who can provide coaching support toward a successful transition.

In many leadership transitions, the greatest friction between outgoing and incoming leaders is more about style than substance. Conflict doesn't occur over what people do but how they do it.

Suppose you and a new owner are fully aligned on organizational goals but choose radically different approaches to get there. You're methodical. You commission research, work the numbers, and watch sales, living and dying with the data. The incoming leader boasts about going with his gut. His instincts tell him what to do.

It emerges that you think your replacement is reckless. Your successor thinks you're slow and overly cautious. Each of you considers yourself a little smarter than the other.

This is really a matter of style, with each approach having upsides and downsides. Besides noting these two extremes need each other, I highlight this an example of a transition issue that might require the assistance of an outside advisor. As a succession coach, I frequently bring departing and incoming leaders together to discuss how the transition is going, including addressing pain points. My clients like having a neutral party guide their discussions.

Succession Watch-Outs

It's no surprise when a transition process causes strain between strong leaders. The best laid succession plans don't always turn out well.

You never know exactly how a transition will turn out.

If you're an owner, you maybe get right to the altar where you're ready to sign papers and be done when your stomach suddenly swims and something inside says, "I don't think so." Those misgivings can happen on both sides. Tension grows, and one or both sides string out the process. You don't want the other person to go away but you're not ready to get married.

Or the same uneasiness can strike when you work closely with your successor through the transition process. You're surprised to feel remorse:

I saw all this talent...
It's not working to hand off responsibilities...

I see cracks all over the place...
I didn't expect this...
I'm invested in this person...
I'm committed...
I have doubts.

Your challenge is to identify issues early and meet them head on. Here are a few critical concerns:

- **LACK OF LEADERSHIP** – As you watch someone step into a new role, you realize she doesn't know what she doesn't know. Or her subject-matter expertise or other credentials covered up her lack of leadership readiness.

- **INCOMPLETE COMMITMENT** – Your successor is trying out the role rather than going all-in. Excitement and a little naiveté convinced him to take the job, or maybe he's just ultra-cautious. But his sub-par engagement puts everything at risk.

- **TEAM CONFLICT** – The rush of power leads your successor to overexert authority. It's her way or the highway. Culture is going up in smoke and employees are fleeing. Vital knowledge, relationships, and accounts might leave with them.

- **CULTURE SHOCK** – Culture changes are pushing talented people out the door, and few people in the market are willing to come replace them. You're not sure if any amount of new talent will keep the business from eroding.

- **OVEROPTIMISM** – Your successor sets out to prove what a wonderful new boss he is, and his missteps will come back to haunt him. Or wishful thinking causes the new leader to overextend financially at a time he should plan for loss of productivity and profit.

- **EXIT** – The most calamitous watch-out is the possibility of complete breakdown of transition. Your successor departs. Or you push that person out.

As I said at the start of this chapter, succession is rife with risks—heightened by these issues and many more. If difficulties between you and your successor loom large, seek help before you reach the point of no return. You'll likely need your full advisory team of accountant, lawyer, and talent management expert to play a part.

Recovering from Breakdown

When succession relationships grow difficult, you face a choice of working it out or parting ways. Sometimes you can reconcile and start fresh with your successor. Sometimes you can't. It's up to you to determine what happens next.

A transition failure will leave you reeling. A crucial first response is to assess damage. In the immediate aftermath, you won't be able to acknowledge or absorb the full extent of the disaster. It's as if you crawled out after a storm and realized your house is gone. Shock takes over. You'll need your trusted advisors to tell it to you straight when you're ready.

Often, a transition failure sets an organization back for years. Internal candidates who were passed over will be justifiably wary of stepping up. Others just aren't ready to fill the void. Cautionary tales will spread quickly to potential external candidates.

When the company's next leader vanishes, the rest of the organization needs calming. If that chosen individual couldn't succeed, how can others think their futures are secure?

Your best immediate hope when succession falls apart is to look for individuals across your organization who have the highest potential to *partially* fill gaps. While others might not be qualified to succeed you, they can take on portions of a role on an interim basis. In your rush to fill gaps, don't promote people unready to lead at a higher level. If you set those people up for failure, you'll create new problems and additional leadership holes to fill. Those who do step up need an abundance of attention and role-specific coaching from an outside resource.

Few leaders who get deep into a transition only to watch it unravel have much stomach for restarting. As a talent management advisor, I see three takeaways that should inform your own path to Succession Readiness:

- **Start working on the steps of Maximum Momentum early, so you have time and energy for mid-course corrections or even to start over.**

- **Take each transition step deliberately, with the guidance of trusted advisors, to preempt as many problems as possible and quickly manage those you can't avoid.**

- **If your organization experiences a transition failure, revisit your values. As you decide what comes next, your legacy matters more than ever.**

When You're Done

There's no secret formula for deciding when your successor is fully prepared for you to leave, except knowing there's no such thing as fully prepared.

Progress against a well-crafted transition plan will indicate your successor's readiness for you to exit. And the date you set for your departure starts a clock ticking. You need overwhelming reason to overrule that.

Whether your temptation is to exit early or to linger, ask yourself what motivates that move. Remember Maximum Momentum: Are you doing everything you can to achieve the best for your company, your customer, and your future? How do your decisions help or hinder those efforts?

In chapter nine, we'll look at your options for staying in the business—or not—after your exit. Before we get there, let's look at how to prepare your customers for the future.

Endnotes

1   Ron Carruci, "Executives Fail to Execute Strategy Because They're
    Too Internally Focused," *Harvard Business Review*, November 13, 2017,
    https://hbr.org/2017/11/executives-fail-to-execute-strategy-because-theyre-too-in-
    ternally-focused (accessed June 1, 2019).

2   Jacquelyn Smith, "4 common reasons half of all new executives fail,"
    Business Insider, March 2, 2015, https://www.businessinsider.com/reasons-ex-
    ecutives-fail-2015-3 (accessed June 1, 2019).

CHAPTER SIX

Customers | Retention

As Roger walked an assembly floor at one of his most loyal customer's, his first stop was a row of machines inspecting precision components. Nearly two decades earlier, Roger had founded a company that designed equipment for testing microscopic mechanical parts. His innovations swept several sectors, with his company's products dominating quality assurance efforts at not only this plant but hundreds of others. Seeing his inventions in the field always intrigued him. An engineer at heart, Roger studied the remaining assembly process, unsurprised by the streamlined flow integrating people and automation to build familiar products in new ways.

Roger's host, the plant's CEO, had awarded Roger his first major contract. Those orders kept the doors open at Roger's startup, yet there was an instance when the account almost evaporated. A new hire at the assembly plant wanted to make a mark by switching vendors, and the CEO personally intervened after product failures jumped. The business came back to Roger and has stayed with him since.

Roger has diversified his company's offerings from engineering test equipment to building and supplying complete test machines and following up with service contracts, giving customers peace of mind and ensuring ongoing revenue to Roger after the sale.

Technology breakthroughs set off periodic cycles of design, implementation, and maintenance. Roger has seen the industry mature, however, and the slowdowns between innovations have lengthened.

Still, Roger was pleased when he sat down with the host CEO and other leaders for an account review. Plans were in place to provide the latest test equipment to additional plants, and no one balked at a price increase. Roger had brought along the senior leader who manages the daily details of the account, but with Roger in the room no one seemed interested in what the account manager had to say. When questions arose, every head turned to Roger for an answer.

Roger concluded that the business relationship was as solid as ever. He had made his company—and himself—indispensable.

Leader at the Center

Maximum Momentum requires transferring knowledge—what your successor must know. But your handoff isn't complete without also transferring relationships—addressing who a new leader must know.

In most organizations, the CEO is corporate ambassador, the face of the business. Moreover, the top leader often plays the role of Chief Sales Officer. While leaders might be important to product development, finance, operations, marketing, and more, they are often inextricable from sales, especially in small- to mid-size organizations. The smaller the organization, the more likely customer loyalty resides with the CEO.

Leaders of larger organizations usually let go of negotiating contracts and rarely manage day-to-day interactions with client businesses, but they command respect and responsiveness when they pick up the phone to talk to counterparts at key accounts. They notice what makes other businesses tick, size up sales opportunities quickly, and act to make deals happen.

Which of these words best describe your own roles with customers? Do you...

- Initiate
- Hunt
- Attract
- Acquire
- Personalize
- Celebrate
- Expand
- Deepen
- Guide
- Advise
- Educate
- Rescue

- Navigate
- Intervene
- Troubleshoot
- Consult
- Fix
- Sell
- Retain
- Upsell
- Negotiate
- Close
- Recruit
- Fire

Whatever roles you fill, you're likely at the center of customer relationships. Your organization rises and falls with your connections.

That's good. And problematic.

For example, a founder often has extensive industry connections and owns many and possibly all customer relationships. Other team members have been siloed in their roles, intentionally or not. If the leader exits, it creates a vacuum. With many parts of the leader's job, others can step in. They can take on new roles. They figure out how to stretch and adapt and lead. But when it comes to transferring relationships, only the leader can do that work. If the leader doesn't do it before exiting, it simply doesn't get done.

Without your intentionally transferring connections, relationships will be lost. Your hard-won accounts become numbers in spreadsheets rather than the faces of real customers. Your successor misses opportunities to revisit, retain, and grow clients. The momentum you've worked hard to build can die, to the detriment of all sides—company, customers, and your own legacy.

External relationships, easily neglected among the rush of pragmatic details, are essential to a thoughtful and intentional transition. You face a choice—making the effort to bridge those relationships or forcing your successor to scramble to recover.

Viability and Value

Retaining customers through your transition and beyond is critical to your organization's long-term viability. In the case of a sale, it's also a key valuation point.

Customers stand at the intersection of three important values:

- **RELATIONAL VALUE** – the friendships you've formed and connections that have advanced your work

- **LEGACY VALUE** – the network that can continue to benefit your organization even after your departure

- **FINANCIAL VALUE** – the additional monetary rewards of passing down a solid customer base

As much as the people, business practices, and products and services you put in place, loyal customers help guarantee the well-being of your organization into the future. Inadequate attention to customer relationships during succession can unravel everything. While it's impossible to quantify the potential damage in your specific situation, the general statistics about customer retention apply:

- Acquiring a new customer costs five times as much as retaining an existing customer.

- The success rate for selling to an existing customer is 60–70%. Selling to new customers, it's 5–20%.

- A 5% increase in customer retention boosts profits by 25–95%.[1]

As an important predictor of an organization's future health, customer retention also forms a key component of business valuation. Evaluators look not only for income derived from diverse customer accounts but from longstanding customer relationships.

All revenue sources are not equal. If acquiring customers requires repeated large spends or you churn customers out the back door as soon as they come in the front, your future revenue isn't as certain as a superficial overview might indicate.

As Wharton researchers point out, historical revenue patterns of two businesses can appear identical while hiding consequential underlying differences. A business with revenue from repeat customers is inherently stronger. Researchers add, "Companies that do a very good job of retaining their customers and developing the value of everybody over time should be awarded a much higher multiple than another business that does not retain their customers as well."[2]

Customer Myths

Long-term, profitable, expanding customer relationships bode well for a company's future. Yet customer loyalty is tenuous, personal, and difficult to transfer.

Consider these five myths about your best customers:

1. Customers are loyal to your brand.

Perhaps—or maybe not. The world's largest companies with the highest brand loyalty know that brand is about a felt personal connection. What if your customers' personal connection begins and ends with you?

2. Customers will tell you the truth about their intention to stay with your company.

When leadership changes, even the most loyal customers are on alert. Even the best-intentioned friends realize circumstances change, sometimes beyond sustainable limits. Can you honestly say you wouldn't feel the same worry if the situation were reversed?

3. Customers you lose are easily replaced.

The numbers don't lie about the expense of acquiring new customers, whether that's a large marketing budget or the efforts of highly-compensated sales people. How many new customers did you gain in the last 12 months? What did it take to acquire them?

4. Repeat transactions equal loyalty.

Customers who keep coming back look loyal. But your wins might be purely transactional and therefore temporary—based on familiarity, convenience, pricing, location, or dozens of other motivators. What happens when you face shifting customer needs and desires or a newly competitive landscape?

5. Solid customer satisfaction scores mean that all is well with your base.

A great Net Promotor Score, for example, might make you want to pat yourself on the back. But it's vital to understand what's behind a number. How did you get there? How can you stay there? How will you consistently up your game?

What's true is that customers don't stay for long with leaders, companies, products, or services they don't trust or like. In retail, for example, 86% of consumers say loyalty is primarily about "likeability." Similarly, 83% of consumers say it's about "trust." [3]

It's safe to assume that at some point in time, your company's existing customers felt confident enough about you as leader and what you've created to become buyers. Their knowing a competent leader is in control builds trust. Over time, customers become familiar with your organization's business practices and form expectations of how things are done. That's the essence of consistency.

Transition upends all of that.

Customer Turmoil

Transition at the top shakes customers, because it puts the vendor-buyer relationship in question.

What happens if the new leader takes the company in a different direction? Or is it more reasonable to ask *when*?

Succession creates angst within customers. *How will a leadership change impact our business?*

> *What will change?*
> *Will our favorite product be cut?*
> *Will we ever see the upgrades we've been promised?*
> *What about new products?*
> *Will we get the same service?*
> *Could we possibly receive better service?*
> *Might employees be too overwhelmed*
>   *by change to be responsive?*
> *How could this ever turn out well?*
> *Do we need to look for a new vendor?*

Suppose a new leader moves a business from an outward-focused, customer-centric, value-added model to an inward-focused, operations-centric, cost-cutting model. Customers eventually feel the results. *What happened? This isn't the same company!*

In the case of sale, new owners arrive with a big bill from buying the business, and it's common that the first thing they do is raise prices. Customers worry about that. *Are you going to start charging us more?*

Or if new owners don't want to raise prices, they save money by cutting the quality. They squeeze the pennies internally, but customers still feel it. *Where did the old standards go?*

Most powerfully, if you as leader were personally involved with bringing in the business, when customers realize you're leaving, their sense of disruption multiplies. *Who will manage our account? What if our business doesn't matter to the new leader? How can we make ourselves heard? Why shouldn't we switch?*

If you don't empower your successor to confirm and continue your business relationships, your organization will end up competing with other vendors as commodities. It's hard to imagine a more predictable and dire threat to customer retention.

Whenever leaders exit, customers see an opportunity to reevaluate the business relationship. Even if they don't leave right away, they nudge the door open. Transition becomes an occasion to shop.

Granted, most customers give new leaders a chance, especially customers who have multiple strong relationships within the organization. But their radar flips on. They're quick to spot changes in product quality, cost, or service delivery, real or imagined. Instead of being relaxed... *this is the way we do business... we've done this forever... we've got a great relationship with such-and-such company...* now they're on alert.

And if you haven't been caring well for your customers and they're already hypersensitive to change, you're even more at risk for customers concluding your transition is a great time to leave.

In fact, some customers have an instant reaction that a leader's unanticipated departure is an automatic reason to go elsewhere. Unless a product or service is truly unique, the uncertainty of what lies ahead is always taken as bad news. Customers reason that they can always come back, but in the meantime, they're better off buying elsewhere.

This reaction is especially prevalent toward publicly traded companies or other organizations with short-term, quarter-by-quarter business models. Customers know a new CEO is expected to come in and make a huge impact right away. They also understand most internal people can't absorb change on that scale. Customers assume whatever happens will be disruptive.

That's not good.

No Assumptions

Customer behaviors are motivated by their feelings about 1) their relationships with your organization's people and 2) their overall customer experience. If you don't address those concerns, don't assume ongoing business is assured.

Owners know that potential buyers love customer contracts. Going to market with a two-year commitment locking in a major customer means your business value just went up. More contracts equal more money. If long-term agreements aren't in place, uneasiness rules. Without those guarantees of future business, buyers wonder if they purchase you on Friday whether your customers will be around on Monday.

In reality, contracts provide only a temporary reprieve. They make customers compliant. They can also make you complacent.

Contracts ensure customers will continue to use your product or service for the duration, buying your organization time to prove it's still worthy. But many customers look no further than the timeframe leading up to a leadership transition, a period they often perceive as a decline. They don't wait around to see what happens next, even if the new leader brings real improvements.

At best, customers subject to contracts go into wait-and-see mode. But already the question is out there. *Do we still want to work with this company?*

As much as you want to think everything will turn out for the best, you really need to be actively in front of those concerns, managing these natural dynamics.

You might think all is well... *we're in good standing... we have deep relationships...* **but you never know what's happening behind the scenes.**

For example:

- The lead buyer at your customer organization, Company A, has a strong relationship with a salesperson at Company B.

- The buyer at Company A always angles for opportunities to deliver business to the friend at Company B.

- If you haven't helped your successor build an effective working relationship with the leader of Company A by the time you exit, you've thrown the door wide open for Company B to grab the business.

Those are the risks of losing key relationships.

During the normal course of business, the fact that your company's identity is intertwined with your own is a powerful strength. But when we talk about customers and transitions, it creates acute risk. Without your intervention, once you exit, the loyalty won't last.

Intentional Customer Management

One big question hangs over every leadership transition. If you went away tomorrow, which customers would be lost?

That begs the next question. If you went away tomorrow, which customers can your organization afford to lose? The answer is probably "not many" or "not any."

Transferring relationships will require a campaign that reaches every customer so no business is lost. Realistically, limits on your time and energy will cause you to focus on a select few. But which ones?

Consider these types of customer relationships. Everyone you do business with falls into one or another.

Customer Relationship Categories

1. **MISSION-DRIVEN**: You like them so much—you don't care if you make money.

2. **MERCENARY-DRIVEN**: You dislike them—but you make so much money you don't care.

3. **MUTUALITY-DRIVEN**: You like each other—and you're each happy with the business exchange.

Few businesses exist to cater to customers in category one. Or at least the number is limited to select friends.

Not many organizations can maintain a book of business full of category twos. The misery is too much. It's unsustainable.

The best businesses are built on a host of category three customer relationships. You trade goods or services for money, and everyone on both sides considers the exchange fair. You like each other enough to do business over and over.

That sounds simple. But which of your customers truly engages with you in a mutually beneficial relationship? Can you name them? List them? How many customers make the grade?

Your best objective indicator of a real-world mutuality might show up in Lifetime Value of a Customer calculations, which includes not only direct revenue but referral business over time. In other words, what you provide to that customer is so valuable that they not only stick with you for the long haul but bring other business your way. I suggest this is where you focus your customer transition efforts.

SIMPLIFIED CUSTOMER LIFETIME VALUE

CUSTOMER REVENUE past 3–5 years	$
subtract ACQUISITION COSTS	$
subtract SERVICE COSTS	$
add NET REVENUE OF REFERRED BUSINESS	$
CLV	$

Play around with those numbers for those you consider your closest customer relationships. Now who makes the grade? Who forms your customer Top Ten?

As you transition from your organization, it's tempting to fill your remaining days meeting with people with whom you've formed deep personal connections. Or those you've known forever. Or those you simply enjoy socializing with. That's natural. But if your goal is to achieve Maximum Momentum for your organization, your customers, and your future, you need to identify these true best customers. Once identified, these are the relationships you must intentionally move from you to your successor. They are your best past customers, and your successor can build the future from there.

There's more to discover about your customer base and more actions to take. But start here.

Endnotes

1   Linda Bustos, "Customer Acquisition vs Retention" [Infographic],
    getelastic, March 6, 2015, https://www.getelastic.com/customer-acquisition-vs-
    retention-infographic (accessed June 1, 2019).

2   "Why Customer Retention Lies at the Heart of Corporate Valuation,"
    Wharton, February 12, 2018, http://knowledge.wharton.upenn.edu/article/
    game-changing-method-valuing-companies/ (accessed June 1, 2019).

3   "What Is Customer Loyalty?" *Rare*, Summer 2016, https://rare.consulting/
    rare-research/loyalty (accessed June 1, 2019).

CHAPTER SEVEN

Customers | Connections

Like a drumstick on a snare, Lisa tapped a pen on her sleek desk, her characteristic sign of uncontained agitation. Whenever the friend on the other end of the phone tried to inject advice, Lisa rebuffed it, prompting the friend to go silent and let Lisa vent.

"This is a nightmare." A year ago, Lisa announced her decision to step down as CEO of the coding firm she had led for the past ten years. Lisa pictured a triumphant slow walk to the exit, celebrating a decade of exponential growth and plotting her next venture. But the board seemed to savor the opportunity to put a new leader in her chair sooner rather than later.

"Where's the respect?" The board overrode Lisa's recommendation of a successor she had groomed for years, instead snatching an outsider from the competition. Everyone suspected the new hire was the CEO-in-waiting, but nothing had been announced. Lisa wasn't convinced the new guy would last. Recognized as an industry thought leader, he had never led an organization. Lisa pegged him as a dreamer, not an achiever. Perhaps an interesting sidekick, but certainly not the superhero the board made him out to be.

"The board picked him, and I'm just along for the ride. He's learning the business better than I expected. But now I'm supposed to give 'Wonderboy' access to all my connections, and I'm not exactly feeling charitable."

Lisa had succeeded as CEO because she could speak business and technology and inspiration. She grasped her client companies' needs and constraints and effectively directed her people in developing custom solutions. Wherever she went, she won friends, and the business grew because of her strong network of fans.

"I've got no time for this. It's not right." Just yesterday Lisa went to a meeting with a client and invited her successor on short notice. There was little time for him to review the project, much less get the full backstory on the organization. Yet Lisa expected him to have instant chemistry with strangers.

"I suppose dragging him in there was my attempt to sabotage him. I admit it. But if he's so brilliant he should be able to figure things out on the fly."

In the meeting, Wonderboy injected a few comments Lisa deemed reasonably insightful.

"And get this. On my way out, the client said, 'Congratulations on the great hire.' I smiled, but I was furious. I'm still burning."

Lisa went silent. But kept drumming her pen.

Opening Up

Even if you bootstrapped your own company, you didn't get here by yourself. Everyone benefits when you lock in relationships between your successor and customers and other external advocates. If you want to fuel Maximum Momentum, share your connections generously.

Opening your collection of contacts can cause an eruption of thoughts and emotions.

You might share your relational capital without hesitation. Or perhaps you're willing to assimilate your successor into the business while walling off your prime external connections. At worst, you struggle mightily to put up with your successor at the office, and heck if you'll take that individual out in public.

Bridging a successor into your network is the most personally intense task of Succession Readiness. If you have years of working alongside your successor, you can predict how things will go. But if you don't know your successor well, you worry about putting your most valuable resources on the line. You risk your reputation. You chance disrupting relationships.

Personal impact aside, you might face significant management challenges around transferring relationships:

- A successor in a honeymoon phase of onboarding has never been put to the test

- A successor came out of nowhere, so you've never seen that person in action

- A successor who has functioned primarily inside now has an external platform

- A successor who has contributed in customer meetings now must take the lead

- A successor's rise or fall impacts your ongoing financial interest

- A lack of financial stake leaves you unmotivated to help

- A contractual obligation forces your compliance

Expanding your successor's relationships serves the greater good. If you're needing a motivational boost, recall the instances when external help kicked off your own business breakthroughs, and consider this an opportunity to give back. Or choose to pay it forward, trusting your successor will one day pass along your generosity. At the least, decide to open your network for the sake of your own legacy. It's an obvious step to achieving the best for your organization, your customers, and your future.

Cataloging Your Network

Bridging relationships starts with identifying and prioritizing the people your successor needs to know. Inventory the contacts who make you successful—and those who get in your way.

Who has made you and your organization what it is? Consider these categories as you create top-of-mind lists of potential introductions. Later, you can expand your lists and do a more detailed analysis. For now, get down obvious possibilities. Mark those who are absolute necessities.

Non-Customers

Setting customers aside for the moment, what outsiders are critical to your company's operation and growth?

- **INDUSTRY ICONS** – leaders known for business results and effective management. What have they taught you? How could your successor benefit from their role modeling?

- **INFLUENCERS** – thought leaders whose opinions sway thinking on a wide range of topics, from strategy and technology to people management and envisioning the future. Who will keep your successor sharp?

- **BUSINESS INTELLIGENCE SOURCES** – people in the know tapped into everyone and everything. How can your successor access the inside scoop?

- **REFERRERS** – contacts who send business your way, a lot or a little, regularly or sporadically. How can your successor continue and cultivate these relationships?

- **TRUSTED ADVISORS** – experts you rely on in accounting, law, talent management, and more. How and when should your successor tap their knowledge?

- **COMPETITORS** – those you admire from afar or those who directly challenge your business. Who should your successor get to know—and what cautions can you provide?

Customers

Whether you have a few customers or a few thousand, again focus your lists on those who are top-of-mind in each category.

- **TOP-TEN CUSTOMERS** – high Customer Lifetime Value companies with whom you do mutually satisfying business

- **RISING CUSTOMERS** – organizations with the most potential for accelerating or expanding purchases of your current or future offerings

- **DECLINING CUSTOMERS** – key accounts on the wane or actively dying. You once counted on them for revenue, but no more

- **UNDERPLAYED CUSTOMERS** – accounts you've ignored for lack of resources

- **FORMER CUSTOMERS** – because relationships broke down or your products or services were lacking, the customer went elsewhere

While it's never enjoyable to disclose a loss of business, don't let your successor be caught by surprise that someone who looks like potential customer was indeed a past customer. Awkward encounters ensue, and everyone looks bad.

Customer Analysis

You might have identified dozens of external connections crucial to your successor's future performance. To bolster customer relationships, your successor needs more than bare numbers. Explain the backstory—the meaning of the financials and the faces behind them.

Transferring relationships is partly data-driven. I don't have to tell you the best way to analyze your numbers and filter for information most important to your successor. I do want to encourage you to do a systematic customer audit that will give a new leader actionable information, meeting as often as necessary to share all you can about your most essential connections.

Start with the raw finances—but don't neglect what those numbers mean:

- What does the customer buy from you?

- What's the purchase timing?

- What's the revenue?

- What's the profit?

- How much does it cost to maintain the account?

- Is the account trending up, down, or flat?

- Is the account current? Does the company have issues paying?

- What are the prospects for continued business?

- What contracts are in place? When are they up for renewal?

- When did we last explore possibilities for new business?

- What business challenges does the customer face that we could address?

- Which additional products or services should they be buying from us?

- What new offerings could we develop for them?

- What prevents the customer from buying more from us?

- How does the revenue potential of this customer compare with other customers?

- Where does this customer rank in our priorities?

- Can we afford to lose this customer?

Behind that financial data are faces that make it happen. Your customer audit should include a thorough relationship audit touching on these topics:

- When did this customer relationship begin?

- Who from our organization was involved at the start?

- What did it take to win the business?

- Why does the customer buy from us?

- Who are the decision-makers and influencers in the customer company?

- What does the customer think we stand for?

- Where do we meet or exceed customer expectations?

- Where do we fall short of expectations?

- When have we struggled with this customer?

- How easily could we be replaced?

- Who in our organization owns the relationship?

- Who else in our organization is connected to the customer?

- How are you involved in this specific customer relationship?

- What risk does your exit pose to continued business?

- What proof exists that this relationship is more than transactional?

- How do we communicate with the customer—and how often?

- Who controls our messaging with the customer?

- Are contracts in place that will buy a successor time to prove themselves?

- Do any reasons exist to end this customer relationship?

Asking and answering these questions will give your successor background essential for relationship continuity. Without your providing these details, your successor could spend months or years getting up to speed. In the meantime, the connection between your organization and the customer will lag, and the business could easily be lost.

The Customer Story

Every customer is part of a larger organizational story. Who are your core customers? How did you acquire them? Why do they stay? You're able to tell the beginning, middle, and present-day story of the organization. Your successor should be able to tell it too.

When departing leaders don't pause to appreciate the arc of what they have accomplished, they lose a chance to affirm and celebrate their own work. They're also unable to pass the narrative down to those who come after them. You're the prime repository of institutional knowledge. Use these questions to pull together the big customer story.

Origins

- Who was here at the start?

- Why was our organization founded?

- What goals did our founders want to accomplish?

- Who were our first customers?

History

- What were our milestones in organizational leadership?

- What companies have been significant customers through the years?

- What new customers have we gained along the way? Why?

- Which customers have we lost? Why?

- What has our ideal customer profile looked like at various stages of our company?

- When have sales and marketing efforts succeeded in adding customers?

- What have we tried that didn't work?

- What do we wish we had done differently in gaining and growing customers?

Present

- How has our organizational mission changed?

- What customers have we added in the past year?

- What is our ideal company profile today?

- Where do customer relationships reside?

- Should customer relationships be distributed more broadly throughout our organization?

- Which customers present obvious or hidden watch-outs?

- Why do customers stay with our company?

- Which customers do we want to keep at all costs?

- What relationships do we need to reinvest in and recover?

- Which customers should we let go?

Those answers sum up how you do business, and they have practical applications. Your big-picture review might say you've done better than you dreamed. Or that you're living on a legacy, with healthy revenue but few significant new customers added of late. Or that you have a segment of high-revenue, high-maintenance, low-profit customers, some possibly more trouble than they're worth. Leverage that information to identify and address issues and educate your successor.

Firing Customers

If you have customers you wish you'd never met, imagine the dreadful reckoning you're setting up for your successor. It's like moving into a house and finding a nest of snakes.

Some leaders never say no to work and never say "Enough!" when customer relationships sour. That lackadaisical approach drains your organization of time, energy, money, and talent. It comes with an enormous opportunity cost. What better things could you accomplish with your resources?

If you've delayed dealing with customers who no longer benefit your organization, now is the time to fire them. Some scenarios:

- **UNETHICAL** – They bend and break the rules, whether legal requirements, ethical guidelines, or industry best practices. It's tough to avoid being painted as guilty by association, and the customer's actions can create legal exposure for your organization. If the situation can't be resolved, a break is required.

- **UNSUITABLE** – They miss the sweet spot of your business model, so you're perpetually creating substantially new offerings to meet their needs. Your people and your P&L will indicate when your efforts are unreasonable compared to what you expend on behalf of other clients. Weigh these customers against the principle that difficult work is better than no work.

- **UNPROFITABLE** – They bring in dollars that result in a negative net. The question is whether that's always been the case... or if circumstances have changed... or if the shortfall can be remedied anytime soon. These customers require a critical analysis to discover any possibilities for serving them profitably.

- **UNHAPPY** – They're perpetually dissatisfied. Or you cringe when you think of them. Or your team wants to quit. The solution might be better boundaries. Or contracts with more explicit expectations. Or something might be broken beyond fixing. Consider the price tag you put on putting up with abuse. When will you say, "Enough!"?

Each of those scenarios is different from customers who make you

- **UNCOMFORTABLE** – They challenge you to be better, and the struggle makes you stronger. These customers are probably worth keeping.

All the statistics about the financial upside of retaining customers don't pertain to counterproductive relationships. That subset of customers won't buy more from you nor bring you referral business. Culling the worst of the worst will increase your successor's ability to focus on better things and increase the likelihood of organizational success.

Customer Data

Ready access to customer data is an assumption behind all my recommendations regarding relationship transfer.

I've assumed you have ready access to this customer data, whether it's all in your head, tucked away in spreadsheets, or safe in a sophisticated CRM tool. Whatever the case, for the sake of your successor, transition requires you to up your game. Three rules:

Get it DOWN – customer information must reside somewhere other than your head

Get it ORGANIZED – the better your system, the better your results

Get it SECURE – information open to the world can sink your company

Capturing data in a CRM system is part of ensuring your legacy. Information that isn't recorded, accessible, and secure doesn't exist. If all your knowledge and relationships go away when you hit the golf course and shut off your phone, your organization is in trouble.

Relationship Transfer — The Process

Many of the problems of succession come down to making explicit everything you carry in your head. Relationship transfer requires information before introductions.

As you put this chapter into practice, you go a long way toward getting customer data out in the open, not only the hard numbers but also your soft-skill knowledge of people. When that information starts to sink into your successor, it's time to focus on helping that person make authentic connections.

CHAPTER EIGHT

Customers | Handoff

"We got the deal done."

"Done?" Dale was surprised. At last report, his protégé, Scott, was holding out for an agreement half a percentage point higher than the customer was willing to pay.

"Bob asked again about our rationale for the pricing," Scott replied. "I walked him through the upgrades since his last major buy, and in the end, he just said, 'I can accept that. Let's go ahead.'"

Hearing the customer had called Scott instead of him, Dale felt a twinge of something inside. The business relationship went back more than a decade, and part of the game was the customer picking up the phone to needle Dale over the final details of a contract.

Dale was pleased Scott won trust as a resource and negotiating partner from a tough buyer.

That twinge Dale felt, he concluded, wasn't jealousy. Was he out of the loop? Yes. Unnecessary? Maybe. But his whole goal was working himself out of a job toward a smooth exit.

This wasn't the first time Dale had groomed a protégé as his successor. A few years back, he was burned by a senior leader who managed upward so well that Dale couldn't help but envision him as his replacement. Dale was making his decision known when it finally became obvious to him that the leader had little support inside or outside the company. Dale had heard about character gaps, but he brushed them off until an industry leader pulled Dale aside and said the protégé wasn't representing him well in the marketplace.

Dale felt positive about Scott as his potential successor, but this time he designed a plan for systematically vetting and developing him inside and outside the organization. And he was much more deliberate in observing, listening, and coaching as the plan played out.

One of the checklists Dale created was titled "Essential Customer Competencies." He would make sure his successor ticked every box.

Customer Relationship Best Practices

To achieve the best for your customers after your departure, your successor must engage the complex range of your customer relationships. There's no shortcutting the process of developing rapport, partnership, and ultimately, trust.

Your successor might be a truly outstanding pick, but without an adequate process for transferring relationships, your business and its customers will suffer.

A successor learning to mimic what made you successful with customers isn't enough. Your organization's next leader needs to connect with customers where they're going, keeping pace with evolving demands. Once again, your job is to coach for the future.

Your customers have formed expectations based on the patterns and organizational systems you've established. If you ask, your customers can provide reasons they keep coming back for more. You could compile your own list of why customers choose you over the competition. Your successor needs you to pinpoint, explain, and model how you do business in the all-important area of customer relationships. What skills do you want to pass along? What practices are so ingrained that you act on them without pausing to think? What are your best tips and tricks for attracting, growing, and retaining customers?

Consider these questions:

How do you...

- Remind the customer of wins and milestones?

- Leverage a consultative approach?

- Listen and really hear?

- Discover unique needs?

- Differentiate your business benefits?

- Collaborate to set goals?

- Invite feedback for improvement?

- Admit when you miss the mark?

- Communicate proactively?

- Communicate regularly?

- Continue the relationship between purchases?

- Use voice, email, text, social media, and face-to-face communications?

- Personalize messaging?

- Reward loyalty?

- Exercise patience?

- Clarify expectations?

- Persuade?

- Challenge?

- Compromise?

- Call the customer to action?

- Share the customer relationship with other team members?

- Expand your organization's network within the customer organization?

- Demonstrate you value each customer and take none for granted?

Understanding your principles is a start. Your successor also needs to know how your general rules apply to specific customers. Expand those potential discussion points with customer skills unique to your setting.

If you've conducted leadership assessments with your successor, you already have a good sense of how that person's readiness, development areas, and derailment risks might impact customers.

I could argue that every leadership competency affects customer experience. But the most relevant competencies cluster around fostering collaboration—proficiencies in good relationships, open dialogue, frequent contact, and no surprises. If your successor puts those to work, customers will feel like they have an effective business partner.

Responsiveness is critical. When customers look to you for a product or service, their world isn't static. If you don't adapt with them as they tweak, reshape, and transform their business, that's trouble. If they change an assembly process, for example, or swap out internal technology, you must flex as well. You can go full steam ahead on your plans, but if they need something else and you don't respond to their requirements, you're a dinosaur. Your business relationship will die off.

Credibility Building

In an ideal world, you begin to transfer customer relationships long before you make a succession announcement. That's easiest in the case of an internal heir-apparent. Whatever the timing, no new leader escapes the need to foster credibility with customers.

Showing up one day and saying, "I'd like to introduce you to my re-placement," is hard on a client. That bolt from nowhere upends the predictable patterns you've established. You shake up expectations, seldom for the better.

If you have time and opportunity to stage the introduction of your successor, consider these steps:

- Start by simply bringing your successor to customer meetings.

- Don't identify your successor as your replacement, although you can give a strong endorsement like, "Scott is my right-hand person."

- Your successor should focus on listening as well as responding clearly and succinctly to questions directed to him or her.

- Over time, make space for your successor to step into more active roles, such as adding to the conversation, presenting, being the first voice to respond, and, finally, leading meetings.

- After you announce your successor, that person should go to key clients and say, "Here's my vision of where we're going."

By that point, you and your successor have tag-teamed to build cus-tomer confidence. Customers will feel reassured that your organization will continue to meet their needs and that your successor won't act radically or otherwise upset a predictable relationship. You'll have demonstrated why customers have relied on you and why they can now count on your successor.

That's a nice transition.

When your successor actively builds relationships with accounts over time, that handoff is likely to be smooth—as long as your successor has developed the skills and experience to take command.

What I'm suggesting is a natural process of building rapport and partnership with customers that culminates in trust. It's the Credibility Pyramid:

THE CREDIBILITY PYRAMID

The Credibility Pyramid illustrates the steps your successor must take to secure customer relationships.

- **RAPPORT ACTIVITIES** are foundational experiences like networking, socializing, and exchanging background and career history. The goal is creating pleasant interactions and finding points in common. The customer feels, "I like this person."

- **PARTNERSHIP ACTIVITIES** are demonstrations of core competencies including listening, learning, resourcing, reviewing accounts, customer education, proposing solutions, and giving and accepting feedback. The client thinks, "I respect this person."

- **TRUST ACTIVITIES** are efforts that build perceptions of higher-level value like strategic collaboration, problem-solving, goal-setting, sales, and follow-up. In the end, the client concludes, "I want to work with this person."

As you manage the transition process, use the Credibility Pyramid to gauge how your successor has progressed with specific customers or with your broad customer base. Where has that individual built rapport... partnership... trust?

Success Metrics

How you measure your successor's customer wins depends on the role you've defined. But your successor's do-or-die objective is to build the rapport, partnership, and trust necessary to mutually beneficial business relationships.

In this context, wins might mean closing transactions. But effective long-term relationships entail more than sales. Early indicators of success might be your successor's ability to work a room, make easy connections with established and potential customers, gain a reputation in your industry, resolve issues for difficult customers, lead calmly in crisis, or simply command attention with executive presence.

One clear indicator your successor is winning is when customers start calling that person for advice. Or when customers look past you in meetings and direct questions to your successor. Those are powerful signs of good chemistry.

Transferring relationships is about the intangibles. If an authentic relationship is developing—characterized by rapport, partnership, and trust—that bond is likely to carry on even when you're not in the room. If you're still working hard in client meetings to maintain connections while your successor sits passively or is ignored, you've got a problem. If, however, your successor is undertaking the hard work of building effective business relationships, then deals will follow.

The Public Hand Off

If you've allowed yourself three to five years to work your Maximum Momentum plan, the question becomes when you should publicly identify your successor. When do you let the outside world know what's happening?

Timing your announcement of your transition has a lot to do with the internal dynamics of your organization. As much as anything, it's a talent management situation.

Suppose you've hired a general manager, and you've worked together long enough that you feel great confidence in that person's capability to succeed you. As you've turned over day-to-day duties to your heir apparent, everything has turned out even better than you anticipated.

- If you rush the process and announce your successor too soon, you increase the likelihood that individual will coast to the position. How will you maintain accountability?

- If you wait too long to name your successor, there's a good chance your standout leader will get impatient and leave. What's the reasoning behind your delay?

- If you're in a situation where multiple people could potentially take your place, as soon as you make your choice, you stifle competition and it's almost certain some candidates will leave. Don't get ahead of yourself. How will you make your decision?

In the case of succession by an internal candidate, where mentoring could go on indefinitely, once you announce your successor, make your exit timeline clear. Plan to stay a minimum of six months and a maximum of twelve. The new leader will have enough time to work into your role, affirm relationships, and close business transactions.

Gaining clarity about your choice, determining the timing of your exit, and even positioning your announcement are all areas where a talent management advisor can help.

Communicating Leadership Change

You've identified your successor and you're ready to announce, whether a sale of the business or just a new leader. Your critical accounts will appreciate a heads-up.

In a larger company, you likely have a public relations professional managing external communications. That person or team with a flair for writing will orchestrate press releases to reinforce continuity and express the company's core values. You'll be quoted sharing credit for your achievements and thanking your team for their friendship and tireless support. Your successor will offer kind words about building on the foundation you've established.

In a smaller company, you might create that announcement yourself.

Either way, the goal is for customers to sense a thoughtful transition is happening and feel secure.

It's your job to decide if a handful of contacts expect that news before it breaks—if you're legally permitted to disclose it, of course. You also need to determine the wider circle of connections that need a call, coffee, or meal within the next couple of days, and a still wider circle to meet with in the coming weeks. List and prioritize people you need to personally call and say, "We've been doing business forever, and I want to say thank you and give you a heads-up. I'm naming so-and-so as my successor."

The last thing you want to do is to surprise key customers. Picking up the phone and calling conveys personal respect.

Your external communication efforts should coordinate with the news you now share with your internal people. In chapter five, we noted the need to widen the circle of trusted advisors and high-level team members aware of your plans, but now you need to drive your message of continuity and values through all layers of your organization. As with external audiences, you want your people inside to sense you've carefully considered every aspect of the upcoming changes, and that all will be well.

The Path Forward

If transferring relationships is the most personally intense aspect of transition for you, that's also true for your successor. As your organization's next leader begins to manage customer relationships, don't expect that person to be your clone.

Of course, you would never say out loud you want a clone.

But you chose a successor with whom you feel chemistry, right? You can relate to that person based on similar experiences and outlook, and your comfort level creates trust. Your successor might even remind you of yourself at an earlier point in time. "Ah," you say, "back when I...."

Your business today doesn't need that younger you.

Say you started the business, or you stepped into the organization when it was smaller. You've grown it over time. You can proudly say that you began with a $4M business that now stands at $150M, with growth projections of 10–20% a year for the foreseeable future.

You might forget how much you've changed. It's difficult to measure your personal growth over time. You've gained extensive skills and knowledge. You probably wouldn't even recognize your younger self.

Your organization needs a different kind of leader to step in and take it to the next level. Someone who starts now and ultimately surpasses you. Not someone who takes you back to the old days.

As you turn over long-standing customer relationships to a new leader, that individual won't be your clone, so filter those expectations. Your successor will create a unique personal way of connecting that can't possibly replicate your own. Whatever the approach, it just needs to accomplish the same goals of rapport, partnership, and trust that lead to mutually beneficial relationships.

As you've come this far, you've worked hard to give your organization and your successor Maximum Momentum. You can have every expectation you will have achieved the best for your company and your customers. Now it's your time to focus on creating your own best future.

CHAPTER NINE

Self|Identity

It had been forever since Meg had dreamed about her days as a college pole vaulter. This time, the stands are packed with friends and allies from across her professional career. As she's done thousands of times before, Meg accelerates with swift, precisely-measured steps. She plants her pole, launching upward and soaring over the crossbar. As her momentum fades, she falls downward, plunges into the crash mat with a satisfying *thomp*—and jerks awake.

Meg pats the mattress to remind herself she's in bed. She blames last night's second glass of wine for the mash-up of college and career, but the dream's meaning wasn't hard to decipher. Months earlier, Meg's company had thrown her a retirement party. She hated the word "retirement," but whatever her "next phase of life" was called, the love and appreciation she felt was unmistakable. The company auditorium was full, and the receiving line lasted until midnight.

As Meg makes coffee and prepares for another day minus the pressure of being CEO, she muses that her last year was a new personal best. Her career trajectory had always been a powerful upward arc, and she certainly finished at the peak, leading a celebrated company to record profits with no end in sight. She had cleared the bar with ease.

Now what?

Meg had planned to get a head start on her next phase of life while she was still in her CEO role, but a booming organization and a complex transition left her as spent as any season of her career. It was impossible to hit pause and envision life after business with any clarity. She has ideas, but nothing as well-considered as she anticipated. People assume she's available, and opportunities for fun and further work are piling up. She's pushing everything off. For the first time in her adult life, she doesn't feel sure about commitments.

Meg is glad she cleared the bar of corporate leadership one last time. But as she sinks into the crash mat, she isn't sure how to get up.

Personal Readiness

As you've crafted your plan for Maximum Momentum, you've prepared your company and customers for your departure. You've ensured the organization will get stronger and outside allies will be well cared for. Now what about you?

The word "retire" comes from a French root meaning to "withdraw" or "retreat." Maybe you equate your exit with retirement, or perhaps the r-word isn't in your vocabulary. Whatever the case, withdrawing and receding aren't likely on your calendar.

Personal Readiness is the crucial third component of Maximum Momentum, achieving the best for your company, your customers, and your future. It's undoubtedly the easiest aspect to neglect. But it's how you accomplish the best for *you*.

Exiting leaders rarely plan for their future with anything near the attention and detailed analysis they bestow on their business. If an underling brought you such slapdash work, you would find it unacceptable.

Without careful thought around what comes next, the future you want will elude you.

Readiness, says the dictionary, means you are

- completely prepared or in fit condition for immediate action or use

- duly equipped, completed, adjusted, or arranged, as for an occasion or purpose.[1]

Reread those words carefully. What leader doesn't want to face the future with readiness? To be ready means you're fit... useful... adjusted... purposeful... equipped... prepared to act.

Personal Readiness isn't a dream or ideal. It's a state to attain, maintain, and execute.

Leading an organization well doesn't happen by accident. Neither does discovering your own path forward:

- Organizational plans are far-reaching. Your personal plans likewise should be holistic.

- Organizational plans align with strategy. Your own goals should embody your highest values.

- Organizational plans provide a roadmap that is directionally accurate—no more, no less. The best personal plans set your course while making room for rethinking and redirection.

Your choices impact not only your own quality of life but that of loved ones. If you fail to make intentional, healthy decisions, others will feel the consequences. These are high-risk moves.

Exit Stages

As you've watched peers step out of leadership and into the rest of life, you've seen some struggle. There's nothing like sitting atop an

organization. Coming up with your next act isn't easy. The toughest spot of all is uncertainty about what to do next.

Every exiting leader goes through predictable stages of optimism, exhilaration, and adjustment. Most expect the journey to look like this:

THREE STAGES OF A LEADER'S EXIT (IMAGINARY)

Those steps are a thrill ride. Lots of ups and downs, twists and turns, but what a rush:

- **ANTICIPATION** – Before you exit, you can't wait to move on to your new life.

- **CELEBRATION** – As you exit, you're amped up and ready for anything.

- **REDIRECTION** – After you exit, you jump into whatever looks appealing.

Actual leadership exits are more stomach-turning than that imaginary ideal. While anticipation, celebration, and redirection do lie ahead, each stage is complicated by conflicting thoughts and emotions:

THREE STAGES OF A LEADER'S EXIT (ACTUAL)

Your actual departure might feel more like this:

- **ANTICIPATION (AND ANXIETY)** – Before you exit, you're like a kid looking forward to the last day of school. What could be better than summer? But in reality, excitement also mixes with concern: "What was I thinking when I decided to be done?"

  You've probably watched exiting peers struggle. Perhaps you've heard stories of leaders who leave one day and get last rites the next. I hear leaders say things like, "If I leave, is it going kill me?" Or "I want to be done, but I don't know what to do next. I don't want to end up dead." Their words are tongue-in-cheek—but not really.

  Your post-exit plans are a critical concern, and wellness research does show that a life without purpose can drastically endanger your health. But awareness of the problem doesn't automatically produce answers. It's easy to let the busyness of transition push back your exploration of next steps.

- **CELEBRATION (AND DISAPPOINTMENT)** – As you exit, make sure you get a party. And then you'll be off to celebrate. For a while, all is probably well. But within a few months, an unsettling question might cross your mind: "Is this all there is?"

  Quick exits make transition especially problematic. You get a too-good-to-refuse offer, and within months, you're lying on a beach. Or you're struck by health concerns or family issues, and you need to get out fast. In neither case do you have much chance to look ahead.

- **REDIRECTION (AND ROUTINE)** – After you exit, you'll start checking boxes of things you always wanted to do. But after a while, you can feel like you're throwing darts in the dark. Nothing fully satisfies. Trying one thing leads to trying lots of things. You become a serial joiner. Or you give up and settle into a dull routine that's nothing like what you imagined the day you decided to be done. You'll wonder, "What now?"

The moment you leave your role, others will line up wanting to fill your time—and take your money. Whatever the circumstances of your exit, others assume it came with a big payday. Without sorting out who you are and what you want to do, you're susceptible to making commitments you later regret.

You don't have to be caught off-guard by these inner conflicts, and they don't have to dominate your transition. They can, in fact, provide motivation to further develop your plan for Maximum Momentum. When your preparation includes directional thinking about your own future, you ensure your own readiness. If something unexpected happens—good or bad—you're still prepared.

As a leader, you probably pay yourself last. That makes the decision to start building Personal Readiness early even more essential. If you cram your transition into a short timeframe, your focus will be preparing the business itself, with its financial complexities and messy people and culture. Your plans will get pushed aside.

Your future deserves to be part of your transition thinking right from the start. Discerning your path forward is best done over time, intentionally, little-by-little, step-by-step.

You don't need to know exactly when you'll leave your role, but with an exit window on your radar, you have time to put systems in place. You can gather people to share the work of a successful transition. And you'll get much-needed space to think about what's next for you.

Rediscovering You

Your dream for what comes next might be to golf until your legs give out, but unless you plan to become a professional golfer, you'll need more. So what will you do?

Before you answer that, there are more basic questions to address.

Leaders often romanticize what they want to do post-exit. On the surface, their ideas sound appealing, but few leaders test those notions with a thoughtful self-evaluation to really determine the best ways to expend their time and resources.

As an exiting leader, you might wonder about *what to do*. Before you answer that, you need to think about *who you are*:

- IDENTITY – Who am I?

- RELATIONSHIPS – Who matters most to me?

- PURPOSE – What do I value?

When you're engulfed in a leadership role, your answers to those questions might be so linked to work that your job overwhelms everything else. Determining answers that fit your new life requires gaining awareness of what you want not just today but for the future, then aligning with what you discover.

Knowing who you are lights your path forward.

You—The Whole Person

For much of your adult life, the title on your door has defined who you are. You're a leader. As you consider what comes next, you need to think more broadly about your identity. You're a whole person.

Many leaders are all business, so focused on the organization that they neglect other parts of their lives. Few make an intentional choice to live a balanced life. Some even boast about their lack of balance.

One-track thinking won't carry you forward. As a complex person entering a radically different new life, it won't fill you up.

For most exiting executives, the transition from leader to ex-leader entails shifting

from **DOING WHAT IT TAKES** for the business
to **WANTING SOMETHING MORE** in life.

Every leader has a unique personal definition of "something more," but for most, leaving an organization is motivated at least in part by a desire to reconnect with family and friends, engage in recreation, improve physical health, learn new things, dabble in deep questions, or all of the above.

Psychologists know that human thriving comes from multiple factors, which they illustrate as a "wellness wheel." [2]

In the jumble of life, your wellness constantly shifts. If you're hit with setbacks or stress in one dimension, you can maintain resilience by keeping other dimensions strong. Overall wellness results in confidence and contentment.

Your transition is a critical pivot point to consider how all the dimensions fit together and how you can thrive in each area.

- **Physical** – Your best health can lie ahead. How will you optimize your physical well-being?

- **Intellectual** – Leading an organization flooded you with information. How will you continue to challenge your mind?

- **Emotional** – A good poker face can't erase whatever feelings you have about leading and leaving. How will you address those?

- **Social** – Your attention is shifting away from the workplace. What will change in how you interact with family, friends, and former associates?

- **Financial** – Your exit has financial implications. What's your plan to manage resources?

- **Environmental** – You're done with long days at the office. Where will you settle in now?

- **Occupational** – You're an expert in leading and making things happen. What will you do with that drive?

- **Spiritual** – You're undergoing a personal revolution. What's life all about?

The point of the wellness "wheel" is that your well-being as a whole person depends on developing in each area. Years of working hard at your occupation might have created gaps in other areas, as if you're driving on bent spokes, bent rims, or a flat tire.

You can rate yourself for each dimension of wellness. A **1** means you struggle with a severe deficit in that area. A **5** or **6** signifies you're doing okay. A **10** indicates you're thriving. Jot brief details about your ranking.

Physical	1	2	3	4	5	6	7	8	9	10
Intellectual	1	2	3	4	5	6	7	8	9	10
Emotional	1	2	3	4	5	6	7	8	9	10
Social	1	2	3	4	5	6	7	8	9	10
Financial	1	2	3	4	5	6	7	8	9	10
Environmental	1	2	3	4	5	6	7	8	9	10
Occupational	1	2	3	4	5	6	7	8	9	10
Spiritual	1	2	3	4	5	6	7	8	9	10
	Struggling								**Thriving**	

For each dimension, what one step could you take to increase your well-being? Of those steps, what are your top three priorities?

As you endeavor to answer the question "Who am I?" today, remember that you're more than your job. Now is your best time ever to fully engage with all of life.

But there's more to who you are. Recognizing you're a whole person—complex and multi-dimensional—doesn't alter the fact that you're always and forever a leader.

You—The Leader

Exiting a position doesn't do away with the occupational slice of your wellness wheel. Your "occupation" is how you fill up your days, and even as your role changes, you're the same person at your core. You'll probably need outlets for your leadership talents.

Leaders vision. Plan. Execute. Create impact. Overcome obstacles. Rack up accomplishments. Keep score.

There are surely parts of leadership you're ready to let go of and never look back. But what about the parts you'll miss?

Your next phase of life will bring fresh opportunities to apply the best of your knowledge, skills, and experience. If you've taken formal assessments of your leadership competencies, that data hints at what you offer.

Consider the leadership themes I mentioned in chapter four and a few of the competencies they comprise. Which themes and competencies especially describe you? Which do you want to keep using?

- **Thinking strategically** – gathers and evaluates information to solve problems, thinks long-term about what's best

- **Building talent** – accurately assesses strengths and development needs; inspires others to commit to challenging goals

- **Fostering collaboration** – relates well across levels, builds trust, communicates well, acts with courage

- **Leveraging change** – looks for new approaches and creative solutions, proactively drives value, learns from experience

- **Driving results** – initiates, organizes, finds efficiencies

Use this basic list and add other competencies you most enjoy using. To make this exercise concrete, compile a list of at least 25 things you do well. Circle the five you do best *and* can envision yourself continuing to do.

Another way to discover and prioritize your leadership competencies is to think back to your accomplishments. When were you recognized for your efforts? When were you gratified by what you did even when no one noticed? Start a list of reminders of your best work. For each, fill out the details: What? Where? When? With whom? Why?

As you reflect on these simple exercises, what do you discover?

For now, you don't need to decide where you might apply these leadership competencies. By pinpointing what you love to do, you'll be ready for what comes as well as confident in your commitments.

In, Out, Or In-Between

You'll likely need to make one decision regarding potential leadership outlets sooner rather than later. What's the nature of your relationship with your organization going forward? Will you walk away—or stay connected in some capacity? And what if any financial ties will you maintain?

You might have no say about your connection to your organization. But if possibilities remain, what are those possibilities? What does the organization want? What do you want?

EXIT   **ENGAGE**

Mark where you fall on that spectrum. Jot any options for how you might stay involved: consultant, board member, subject matter expert, ad hoc leader, informal advisor, or....

How much time and energy will you give your organization? On what terms?

Note that it's highly difficult for organizational founders to stay involved. Many have moved into roles where they offer ongoing input, but few succeed. There's just too much temptation for founders to overstep boundaries.

Your connection to your organization might be financial as much or more than relational. Will you completely divest of any ownership or financial involvement, stay fully invested, or something between?

DIVEST   INVEST

Be aware of conditions that come with your ongoing involvement in whatever form, at whatever level. What are the obligations spoken or unspoken with your commitment? How do those obligations impact other areas or other people in your life?

Getting There

Reflection feels like a luxury while you're in the business, but it's a necessity you can't afford to go without. Maximum Momentum requires pausing to think not just about your organization but about yourself.

You need to understand your past and present before you can determine your future. Looking backward and forward requires three crucial attitudes:

- **COURAGE** – to honestly assess where you're at personally. Just as you audit your business for gaps that require repair, evaluating the non-work aspects of your life will point you to places where you can truly thrive.

- **OPENNESS** – to explore what comes next, without preconceptions. By the way, your current staff likely doesn't want to hear about your process of discovering your next steps when they still need you to lead the company, meaning you typically can't have these discussions inside your organization. Lean on your external trusted advisors.

- **ADAPTABILITY** – to keep at your pursuit of meaning and purpose. You don't have to know exactly what you're going to do when you leave, but you can be directionally accurate about what you want to try. Then flex. What you do the first year might not be what you the second. Your decisions will evolve.

Whatever comes next for you impacts not only yourself but other people. What relationships will you prioritize in your next phase of life? That's the second great question to answer as you explore.

Endnotes

1   *Dictionary.com*, https://www.dictionary.com/browse/ready (accessed June 1, 2019).

2   Bill Hettler wrote *The Six Dimensions of Wellness* in 1976, defining human well-being in a hexagon shape of six domains: Physical, Emotional, Social, Intellectual, Spiritual, and Occupational. Others have recast his theory as a wheel with countless variations. Peggy Swarbrick developed Eight Dimensions of Wellness, adding the Financial and Environmental domains.

CHAPTER TEN

Self|Relationships

Han slouched into a folding chair on the sideline of his son's preseason scrimmage. Lacrosse was new to him, and he tried to make sense of the game. It looked like a good opportunity for 14-year-olds to put on helmets and a few pads and hit each other with sticks.

Han was glad whenever the referee stepped over to parents on the sideline and explained the rules. But he was preoccupied with other concerns. Han left his firm three weeks earlier as part of a buyout, and the cash in hand bought him freedom to pursue work on his own terms. He wanted a break from running a company and thought interim gigs as a strategic leader might keep him engaged.

All Han really knew was that he felt too young to say he was completely done. One priority was to redouble his efforts to be a better dad, but that was proving tough. His phone constantly buzzed with team members who wanted to process what just happened at the firm. Few were in Han's position of taking an indefinite period to find work, and he was coaching several leaders through their job search. Advising people was what he did, and availability his brand.

Sure, Han was driving his son to and from school and cheering from the sideline, but the last time his son shot and scored, he was checking his phone.

Relationship Turmoil

Leaders looking for "something more" as they exit often put a high priority on relationships, giving fresh attention to family and friends. But many get caught off-guard by the relational adjustments they encounter.

If you're no longer the business owner or CEO, what are you? What identity do you want to nurture?

Transition is a prime opportunity to take stock. If you see yourself holistically, assessing each dimension of your life for strengths and gaps, you're likely to renew your commitment to engaging with people. You don't want to lose work friendships. And you want to strengthen family connections. You find new meaning in saying, "I'm a friend." "I'm a mentor." "I'm a spouse." "I'm a parent." "I'm a grandparent."

But you're not the only one navigating a transition.

Your family, friends, and work associates are also experiencing change. Exiting your leadership role for whatever comes next means your relationships will never be the same. Priorities shift. Expectations adjust. Commitments realign.

At work, for example, the countless hours you logged with team members across your organization made colleagues extremely important to you. Suddenly you have little or no contact. When you don't see or talk with former work associates regularly, you might be shocked at the speed the bonds fade.

So you reach out to connect. You discover people don't snap to attention like they did when you were their boss. Now that you don't sign their checks, they don't put as much weight on what you say. The same falloff can occur with external contacts. When you were CEO and made a call to share tickets for a ballgame or concert, people picked up the phone right away. Now days pass before you hear back.

If most of your relationships originate with your company—your friends are vendors or other industry contacts—leaving puts you in a difficult spot.

Family dynamics can be even harder than turmoil with colleagues. If you have a spouse and children—still at home or grown and gone—your transition changes pretty much everything.

Your transition might be the most chaotic period of your career. You ponder things you've never had to think about. You orchestrate transactions you've never had to direct. More than ever, work might consume you. Then suddenly you're done. The day after your exit, you might wake up late and lounge in your pajamas while the rest of the world goes to work. That's as new for your family as it is for you.

If you're like a lot of leaders, you hit the road to ease the transition. Planning a trip gives you something to look forward to and staying busy keeps you blissfully distracted from the monumental life-change you've undertaken. Travel can be a healthy tactic to ease your immediate adjustment.

But what happens after the trip?

That's when things can fall apart.

If you have a spouse, the pressure on your partner can be overwhelming. That person wants to be supportive, with empathy born of an understanding of the enormous adjustment you face. But your spouse probably isn't well-equipped to handle the situation. You get support... support... support... until your spouse has had enough.

Tension flares. You say things like, "I thought you wanted me to be done!" If you haven't yet wondered whether exiting your organization was a mistake, you do now.

If you have children still at home, you perhaps start showing up at events you often missed. Or maybe you're present for more discussions and decisions, and you inject your opinion where you might not be wanted. Even adults need to figure out how they fit into your transition.

It's not you. Not *all* you, anyway. It's predictable relationship dynamics. It's hard to adjust. It's worse if you don't see these stressors coming and get ahead of them.

Recalibrating Family Relationships

As you navigate a transition alongside your significant others and children, three issues come front-and-center: closeness, control, and cost. To reduce potential tensions and friction as you move forward, you need to reestablish your relationships on new terms agreeable to all sides.

You can get there by asking and answering some basic questions:

RECALIBRATING FAMILY RELATIONSHIPS

Closeness	Control	Cost
When do we want to be together—or apart?	How do we make decisions?	How much do we spend?

Each topic deserves extended discussion with the most important people in your life. While these questions always apply to any close relationship, they're especially relevant during this transition as you grapple with new ways to relate to your spouse and children. The goal isn't to negotiate a contract but to arrive at a mutual understanding.

CLOSENESS—How do we balance time together and time apart?

If you want a relationship reality check, start with some quick math on your typical schedules for the past few years. On average, how many waking hours a week did you and your significant others spend together? Then calculate how many waking hours a week you *could* be together post-exit if you spent all your discretionary time with each other. There's probably a world of difference. So what will you do with your windfall?

Rather than attempting to designate a rigid minimum or maximum number of spousal or family hours, start brainstorming:

- things we already do together

- things we already do on our own

- things we like to do together that we never find time for

- things we want to try together

- things we each want to try alone

Every couple (and family) has a different ideal of togetherness. Think hard about what works for each person involved in your discussion. How can you turn your brainstormed ideas into reality?

The key is talking through possibilities rather than bumbling into situations no one enjoys. The clash of unspoken expectations is bound to leave people hurting. Get each person's needs and wants out in the open.

As the exiting leader, recognize that your desires aren't the only relevant facts in the room. Your spouse might be occupied with a job or other interests. Your children might be booked solid with activities. No one can be forced into this new stage. Ease in.

CONTROL—What's our process for decision-making?

As a leader, you spent your career making decisions that impacted your employees and their families in the present and far into the future.

For people who relied on you for their living, your decision-making prowess made dreams come true. That's heady stuff.

Then you're done. You're at home, maybe a little mopey, trying to figure out what to do with yourself. And nowadays whatever decisions you make seem insignificant in comparison to your old life. The consequences don't carry the same weight.

A lot of leaders miss that impact and attempt to fill that void by exerting authority over their significant others. They start managing the household in potentially negative ways even if they haven't been around much in the past. That's a relationship red flag.

You might need to rethink the decision-making patterns you honed as a leader. Consider how you've included or excluded loved ones from the ups and downs of work, perhaps even your decision to exit. Have you made plans independently—or have you included your spouse in your deliberations, with regular updates on your thinking? Have you simply announced your intentions—or have you asked for input beforehand and built a habit of collaboration?

Some leaders keep work at work. Compartmentalizing is their philosophy of life. Others let their spouse in on everything. That person knows what's going on and understands how you think.

If you've established a pattern of inviting questions and letting your partner share his or her own thoughts and feelings, keep that up. If you've been more private and your spouse has trusted you to just take care of stuff, then you might need to build new habits of communicating and collaborating in this next phase of life.

A need for command-and-control gets at the heart of how you do relationships. It doesn't work well at home. Consider these questions:

- What decisions do you currently face as a couple or family?

- How have you made similar decisions in the past?

- How have you shared decision-making power—or not?

- How can you ensure you and your spouse both feel heard as you make decisions?

- How will you alter your decision-making patterns for this next season?

- When and how will you address this topic with your spouse?

Changing established decision-making habits takes time. Everyone involved needs to feel safe voicing input and confident that input will affect outcomes. But the benefit will be a process you can apply across all of life.

COST—How will we right-size our spending post-exit?

Exiting an organization might mean you finally get to fulfill your lifestyle dreams. If you leave as part of a buyout or you sell a business, others might assume you're suddenly rich. Whether or not that's true, your departure likely brings some level of change to your financial status.

That shift might come at a time when you're making financial plans ranging from traveling the world to getting kids through college or caring for elderly parents. Or choosing to upsize or downsize vehicles, recreational activities, and living spaces.

Right-sizing will impact yourself and others positively or negatively. If you already have a finely tuned spending plan, congratulations. Most people don't. If not, you'll need time to analyze income and expenses and chart your course.

As you adjust to a new financial reality, here's a simple tip to apply immediately. If a spouse is involved in spending choices, consider setting a dollar amount you each can spend without informing the other, a number likely lying somewhere between the cost of a candy bar and a car. Whatever it is, promise to consult each other for anything higher. It might make more sense to set a monthly sum.

If you've cashed out stock or sold a business, your children might have more questions than you realize. If there's been a good payout, the kids start to speculate:

- "Will we see any of this?"

- "Are we going to inherit anything down the road?"

- "Can I quit saving for my kid's college because grandpa and grandma are going to pay for it?"

You might not want to go there. But from now on, those questions and expectations will always be in the background. While initiating money discussions can cause tension, leaving the topic unaddressed can create far worse.

Or maybe your payout wasn't as big as others think. You've got enough to make it, but when you go to meet your maker, you'll need your last dollar to pay for the funeral. Your kids need to understand that.

By the way, "They'll read the will and figure it out when I'm dead" isn't a solid plan.

Conversations let everyone know where they stand. The more openly and regularly you can talk about money, the less weird or disruptive those discussions feel.

If you're going to give everything to charity, let people know that early on. If the wealth you can share is limited, frame your conversations around values. Like, "I value education, so I'd love to contribute to college for the grandkids. Beyond that, there isn't going to be anything else."

Like it or not, money has already injected itself into your relationships. It's up to you to determine what comes next.

Start Now

Leaders who make successful transitions cultivate strong connections outside of work. They prepare for the shifting relationship landscape that lies ahead.

Investing yourself in family and non-work friends is obvious. But your work relationships don't have to end with your exit.

Picture a leader creating a timeline for succession. He's been hugely successful in his business and feels good about the wealth he created and all the things he owns, yet he's pushed away all the people in his life. At work, even his closest connections are just acquaintances. His wife is the only person he really talks to, yet there are limits. For years, he's been an absent partner, and he can't go home and run the household like he runs his business. Reinserting himself into the relationship and trying to take charge will cause genuine strain.

This leader faces a choice. Does he work hard at slowly recovering relationships, or does he carve out a life without people?

You don't have to be that guy—or gal.

It pays to imitate the habits of leaders particularly good at maintaining relationships. They make business connections part of their informal network, taking time periodically for breakfast or lunch. When colleagues move on, they maintain ties. Over time, these relationships morph. Business isn't the only topic on the table. Discussing other aspects of life becomes at least as important.

These leaders also prioritize involvements that foster meaningful relationships. They might sit on the board of a faith community or a nonprofit or another company. They have something to share and people to share it with.

Your next phase of life can be rich with relationships if you proactively decide this is a dimension of life where you want more.

Just as you create a business plan for a new venture, you can create a relationship plan to go to the next level. Use the tables on the following pages to help you prioritize family, friends, and work connections. The idea is simple. Include:

- The person's name

- How you anticipate your relationship will change after your exit

- Your relationship goals (expressed qualitatively, like "more open and honest," or quantitively, in terms of time, frequency, or activities)

Don't feel obligated to fill every line in each table or to complete them all at once. Start with the people who matter most to you and use these pages as your long-range idea list.

FAMILY

	Name	Anticipated Changes	Goals
1			
2			
3			
4			
5			
6			

Non-Work Friends

	Name	Anticipated Changes	Goals
1			
2			
3			
4			
5			
6			

Work Friends

	Name	Anticipated Changes	Goals
1			
2			
3			
4			
5			
6			

Don't Go It Alone

Let's talk worst-case scenario. Throughout your career, you chose being a provider over being present. You wish you could do things over, and a major motivation behind your transition is creating time for family. But once you make the shift, all you get is hostility.

You might feel your career has been a trade-off between impossible choices. You've carried burdens, and your family has felt the load too. Maybe your spouse is frustrated and your children distant. You did your best, but you admit you were far from perfect.

A dynamic that grew over years won't be fixed in a day. Your family probably isn't interested in hearing you grovel over letdowns from the past. What they want is your consistency in the present. They want to know who you are today and why they can rely on you. Talk won't convince them. Actions will.

Your transition might be an extended period of getting reacquainted. If you find yourself continually running into resistance, get help. A counselor with a specialty in marriage and family can help you analyze the situation and coach you through your best steps.

Reconnecting with loved ones is one of the great gifts of exiting a leadership role. Along with feelings of loss comes a new sense of purpose. That's the last piece of developing Maximum Momentum and the topic of our final chapter.

CHAPTER ELEVEN

Self|Purpose

Every head at the senior prom turned as Joe strolled in, the only guy in the ballroom with a date on each arm.

Joe was one of several friends who stood with their classmate Adam through the battle of his life. As an aggressive cancer raced through his body, Adam demanded his friends not let his illness spoil their final year of high school. So when Adam passed away on the morning of prom, it was fitting that Joe show up to the dance with his own girlfriend on one side and his best friend's on the other.

Forty years later, Joe was winding down an impressive career as a technology leader. As he considered his exit, he established three personal goals: 1) reinvest in family and friends, 2) stay connected to innovation, and 3) discover a volunteer opportunity leveraging his leadership skills.

After his exit, Joe began making the most of his new flexibility to be present for his loved ones. He found outlets for his technology expertise in consulting and speaking. And a chance opportunity to volunteer reconnected him with one of his life's monumental experiences.

Unaware of Joe's backstory, a friend gave Joe a business card picked up at a networking event, along with an offhand "I sat next to a guy building a new board. Maybe it would interest you." A few meetings later, Joe was recruiting CEOs to battle cancer through employee health initiatives, fundraising, and legislative action.

As Joe steps into the next stage of life, his days couldn't feel more consequential.

Moving Forward

No one can tell you what you should do next. But figuring *what to do* and *why* is the secret to a satisfying future. Your leadership legacy will always matter. What lies ahead can be just as significant.

The more your identity has been linked and limited to your leadership role, the more likely you are to struggle to let go. It's challenging to move forward if you're constantly looking back. Meanwhile, you have a new life to create.

Financial planners distinguish three phases of retirement, a point that's relevant even if you equate retirement with being put out to pasture or believe your best future is to never quit working. The three stages:

- **The Go-Go Phase – You're on the move.** You're ready to travel, spend time with your grandkids, relaunch into work, or whatever.

- **The Go-Slow Phase – You're decelerating.** You don't do anything as fast as you once did. Health issues, a sick spouse, or lack of resources may slow you down.

- **The No-Go Phase – You're coming to a halt.** You encounter limitations, like lack of mobility. You face real-world choices about what you can and can't do.

Can you Go-Go for ten years? Or does something intervene so that stage only lasts a year?

How long each phase will last is an unknown. But research shows that people live longer, enjoy better health, and feel more satisfaction if they find a sense of meaning. Having purpose results in positive outcomes including improved sleep, fewer heart attacks and strokes, and a lower incidence of disability, dementia, and premature death.[1]

Purpose Versus Activity

Activity fills time. Purpose fills you up. If you want Maximum Momentum as you launch into your future, purpose is how you get there. So what's the difference?

> **ACTIVITY IS MERELY BEING IN MOTION.**
> **PURPOSE IS MOTION WITH MEANING.**

You didn't come this far in work and life to lower your standards on what it means to truly live. The drive that fueled your organizational achievements doesn't go away. After your exit, that energy just propels you in other directions.

When you live with purpose, you're intentional. Your days, months, and years align with what matters most to you. You experience a sensation that you're accomplishing more than staying busy. At some level, you feel you're doing what you were meant to do.

Post-exit, you might plan to go to the club every day and play tennis or racquetball or poker. It's not that activity is bad. Or that it isn't fun. But activity without purpose is insufficient. It's probably unsustainable. It's why even your favorite pastimes get old.

Filling time doesn't quench your human need for something more. If you don't find a way to fill up, you'll face psychological pain. You'll look for a way to dull that hurt, even if you aren't aware of its cause.

Drugs, alcohol, gambling, prostitutes, whatever—it's why even great leaders go astray.

We all need a sense of meaning.

Values

There's no one-size-fits-all purpose out there. It's not all about non-profit volunteering. Purpose comes from discovering and doing what you value most.

You might enjoy several things that feel important. Those passions might shift over time. You might do *this* for a while, and you find it meaningful. And then you discover *that*, and you give it a go. That's fine. What gives you purpose is very personal.

To make the shift from activity to purpose, you need to name and claim your core values. That happens through a process of reflection, discussion, and testing.

REFLECT   DISCUSS   TEST

Reflect

As a leader, you spent your days thinking about the state of your organization and the needs of others. Finding time to discern what really matters to you is tough when you're buried in the business.

Nevertheless, reflection is a powerful tool to slow down and consider where you've been and where you might head.

Here are a couple ways to reflect on your values.

- **CAPTURE YOUR STORIES** – You gain perspective whenever you recall your history. At the time, you were so immersed in work that you might have missed the milestones, the key successes and crucible moments that made you who you are. You might have plaques and pictures to commemorate accomplishments, but the challenges you faced and your determination to push on are just as important to remember.

Consider these questions:

- What were your key successes?

- What major difficulties did you overcome?

- When did you lose?

- What mattered most to you before, during, and after those experiences?

- What do your wins and challenges say about who you are as a person?

- What small daily habits seem significant in hindsight?

- When did you feel the greatest sense of meaning and purpose?

Every leader has epic stories. It often isn't until someone prompts you that you think, "Yes, I got the business through that." Look back and feel good. To solidify your takeaways, pause and remember.

- **CLARIFY YOUR VALUES** – Coaches and counselors of all kinds use "values sort" exercises to help clients discover what matters most to them. Use the following list of values to see what surfaces for you.

Using the words below, circle a maximum of 15 values **important** to you. Star a maximum of five that are **very important**. Rank at least your **top five** in order of importance. Add words of your own for any key values missing from the list, and feel free to make copies for your own use or to invite loved ones to do this exercise on their own and compare what you each discover.

Achievement	Friendship	Personal Growth
Advancement	Generosity	Physical Fitness
Adventure	Happiness	Popularity
Advocacy	Health	Power
Authenticity	Impact	Predictability
Balance	Improvement	Prestige
Challenge	Independence	Quality
Civic Commitment	Influence	Recognition
Competence	Integrity	Relaxation
Competition	Joy	Responsibility
Control	Justice	Safety
Cooperation	Learning	Service
Creativity	Location	Spirituality
Education	Love	Stability
Efficiency	Loyalty	Success
Equality	Luxury	Tolerance
Fairness	Mental Health	Tradition
Family	Nature	Variety
Financial Security	Organization	Volunteering
Flexibility	Peace	Wealth
Freedom	Perseverance	Winning

When an activity aligns with your highest values, your sense of purpose intensifies. Without good alignment, it's likely an activity that won't satisfy you long term.

Discuss

Wisdom says it's not a good idea to ponder values in a cave and then emerge to tell others—like your spouse—what you decided. It's amazing how many leaders buy a business or take a job in another city and then go home and inform a partner without any prior conversation. How does that go over?

Values become clearer with input from others, especially when values drive major life decisions that impact more than yourself. In other words, conversations matter, especially discussions that happen over time and give participants space to process, respond, and ask questions.

To level the playing field, invite others to explore their own values through the reflection exercises above. Then have conversations about what matters to you broadly and how values might impact impending decisions.

You and your spouse, for example, might discuss

- What values do we share?

- What values do we differ on?

- What does a specific value mean to us?

- How will our values shape our lifestyle?

- How do we want to live out our values in a particular situation?

Your transition will be easier when you understand your values, because you know where to invest your time, energy, and money. Whatever the commitment, values make it clearer.

Test

Even if you think you know exactly what your future holds, now is the time to put all your options on the table. Barring pressing health or financial limitations, you're entering a new realm of possibilities. You decide when and where and how to act on what matters to you.

Finding your purpose isn't abstract. You can verify your discoveries through experimentation, exploring options to discern how well they align with your values.

Values are a personal choice. So are the structures you use to frame them. Consider all the different shapes and sizes of what might come next for you:

- **STAY IN THE GAME—Keep working.** A love of work, a financial need, or another compelling reason can keep leaders on the job in one form or another—board work (see below), consulting, interim leadership roles, or full-time employment. A new setting might let you explore interests or scale back and reset boundaries better suited to your next phase.

- **PLAY AT WORK—Keep score.** Some leaders exit with enough money for a lifetime and leftovers to share. But even as they transition out of one role, they can't wait to move to the next. Maybe their thing is putting together new companies. Or solving problems at existing organizations. The money they make isn't about funding a lifestyle. It's a way to keep score.

- **WORK AT PLAY—Sell flowers.** Each spring, one executive bought annuals from the same pop-up gardening center. Now she sells plants six weeks every year, sharing tips with people who share her passion. The social outlet is exactly what she wants, and "working at play" is about something other than making a living.

- **ADVISE—See you at the board meeting.** Board involvement is a perfect opportunity to share accumulated knowledge and experience, like a chemist who gets involved in STEM education. Other leaders become mentors to younger executives or owners. Board leadership and coaching might or might not come with a paycheck, but they often combine components of generosity, staying fresh, and connecting with people.

- **PLAY HARD—Sail the world.** Some leaders really do choose to sail the world or see the country from the driver's seat of an RV. Those who are motivated by distinct values have a ball. The others get bored and wander home.

- **NEST—All about family.** Many leaders express satisfaction at reconnecting with family or building new relationships with grand-children. That sense of meaning signals they're acting on their values rather than fulfilling an obligation.

- **BOOMERANG—Get back in the fray.** Then there's the owner who sells a business and buys a coffee shop. A value around a simpler life clashes with a need for challenge, and the leader sells the shop and buys back the original business. That boomerang doesn't hap-pen often, but it's caused by a lack of clear purpose throughout the transition process. It reflects a trial-and-error approach rather than intentionally figuring out what's meaningful to you.

As you test your values in real life, the questions to answer are simple:

- What's working?

- What's not working?

- What values drive this activity?

- What's missing?

- How can I tweak the experience to better align with my values?

- When is it time to try something else?

Finding Your Purpose

As you explore options, you'll quickly confirm that what you do is important, and why you do it matters even more.

Each time you reflect, discuss, and test activities for alignment with your most important values, you gather data not only about what fills your days but fills you up. You'll find your way to a renewed feeling that you're doing what really matters.

With a sense of purpose, you will thrive in the next steps of life. As Viktor Frankl wrote in *Man's Search for Meaning* (1946), "Everyone has his own specific vocation or mission in life... Therein he cannot be replaced, nor can his life be repeated. Thus, everyone's task is unique as is his specific opportunity to implement it."

Endnotes

1   Dhruv Khullar, "Finding Purpose for a Good Life. But Also a Healthy One," *The New York Times,* January 1, 2018, https://www.nytimes.com/2018/01/01/upshot/finding-purpose-for-a-good-life-but-also-a-healthy-one.html (accessed June 1, 2019).

Epilogue

Picture yourself sitting down for a one-on-one conversation with a younger you—a much younger self getting ready to launch into the great unknown.

If you could package up all the benefits of your life's experience and offer yourself some hard-won advice, you might say something like this:

- **Live up to your values.** The best plans and dreams begin and end with thoughtfully determining what matters most to you. From brainstorming ideas to evaluating outcomes, intentionality rules. Doing what you value most is the secret to finding purpose.

- **Draw on your resilience.** You've already navigated transitions with family, school, and friends. You've surmounted obstacles to get to this point. Tools already in your possession will help you stay focused and move forward.

- **Get help.** If you expect others to do the hard work, you'll achieve nothing. But if you don't get help when you need it, you'll fall short of your goals. Each time you face a new challenge, you learn anew how to get and give assistance.

- **Look forward.** Without careful thought around what comes next, the future you want will elude you. Your past makes you who you are, but the person you become depends on living fully in the present with an eye toward the future.

By pursuing Maximum Momentum, you've done all you can to ensure the ongoing success of your organization and its customers. As you exit your leadership role for what comes next, you launch once again into the unknown.

You could do worse than to take to heart whatever best wisdom you would impart to a younger you, because the change you're experiencing is as substantial as any of your leaps of the past.

As an accomplished leader, you have one more essential bit of advice to consider:

- **Lean into your legacy.** With a host of accomplishments to look back on, you now have time and freedom to consider what more you can add to your legacy. Exiting well isn't your last great act. It's a base to build on, a personal new beginning.

So where else will your leadership drive take you? How can you continue to add value? What else do you want to be known for?

Leaders who make time to envision their future don't let circumstances determine their path forward. Your best transition will happen when intention meets execution, going out on top with energy for what's next.

I wish you the best as you move forward with confidence and clarity.

Acknowledgements

The creation of this book would not have been possible without the extensive support and guidance of my book mentor, Kevin Johnson, an accomplished author in his own right. Kevin contributed in significant ways to the contents of this book as well as provided me with meaningful guidance on how to develop and publish it. I will be forever grateful to him for his willingness to share his wisdom and expertise with me.

I appreciate, too, the contributions of Mickalene Thomson whose organizational skills and typing prowess were invaluable in putting thoughts to paper. Richard Dodson and his team at Artisan Digital were instrumental in orchestrating the design and publication of this book. To each of you, I am grateful.

The clients who have allowed me to be part of their lives and businesses for over 25 years deserve special mention here. Every day they teach me something new about what it takes to build a successful business, and they inspire me with their grit and determination to do so.

Most importantly, I wish to thank my loving and supportive wife, Susan, and my three amazing children, Lauren, Olivia, and Claire. You give me purpose.